MW00907795

On the Receiving End

A Collection of Works for Realizing the Potential Within Ourselves

Monica Davis

American Literary Press, Inc.
Five Star Special Edition
Baltimore, Maryland

On the Receiving End

A Collection of Works for Realizing the Potential Within Ourselves

Library of Congress
Cataloging in Publication Data
ISBN 1-56167-357-9

Library of Congress Card Catalog Number:
97-071575

Published by

American Literary Press, Inc.
Five Star Special Edition
8019 Belair Road, Suite 10
Baltimore, Maryland 21236

Manufactured in the United States of America

Dedication

This book is dedicated to those men and women, young and old, who constantly find themselves on the receiving end of the selfishness, thoughtlessness, and negative actions of others. May you find it to be an inspirational tool in your daily life.

To Audrey Cobb;
Thank you for your support.
Marc [illegible]

Table of Contents

Other Poems of Thought and Inspiration:

Preface

To all who read this book: Although this book portrays troubled relationships and how the parties handled them, I hope that it becomes a confidence builder, morale booster and an attitude enhancer for those who read it. It is meant to provide a common sense and lessons-learned approach.

Don't allow anyone to demean you, disrespect you, diminish your character, or use you for their personal gain. These are all forms of negativity. Regardless of race, nationality, or background, we all face the same problems.

Many of the problems noted herein may seem minor, but to those who experience them, they are not. Minor problems can become complicated.

To protect their identity, the names of the contributors have been changed.

You may not be able to relate to all or any of the cases within, but whatever odds you may be facing, don't give up, your situation can change for the better.

Acknowledgment

First, Thanks To The Almighty.

Special thanks also goes to:

BND, who made time to offer her invaluable assistance.

I also want to thank collectively those individuals who have unselfishly allowed me to use their experiences as a way to express to others that they're not alone and that their problems can be solved.

Warning - Disclaimer

The opinions expressed in this book are from a layman's point of view and are not of a professional nature and are not to be deemed as such.

This book is designed to provide insight in regard to the subject matter covered. It is sold with the understanding that the publisher and author are not engaged in rendering professional services. If legal or other expert assistance is required, the services of a competent professional should be sought.

The purpose of this book is to educate. The author and publisher shall have neither liability nor responsibility to any person or entity with respect to any loss or damage caused, or alleged to be caused, directly or indirectly by the information contained in this book.

On the Receiving End

We've all shared the negative forces
that others cast at us;
we often wonder why some think
that what they do is just.

Some of us will tolerate it
and we tend to make excuses;
for the negative attitudes and undertones
that simply have no usage.

When we open our mouths to speak
let us think before we do so,
for no one wants to be
on the receiving end,
of such harsh negative blows.

Just because they've been done unto,
it doesn't make it right
for them to feel justified,
to pass it on to you.

For you too are human,
just as they are;
you deserve a better life
than one of permanent scars.

If they too were on the receiving end
of such negativity;
they too would want peace of mind
away from those who deliver it.

Some may do it for release;
some may do it for control,
though they know it cold;

others may do it to intimidate
but they all should look deep
within their souls.

The harsh words they speak
can lay like heavy rocks on our minds;
and the only way some can lift them,
is by finding someone less unkind.

Some that do it will say they're sorry,
and they will truly mean it;
but for those whose actions become repetitious,
it's simply just demeaning.

Chapter One

Is It Just Me?

How many of us have often said, "Is it just me that's being treated like dirt?" Sometimes we become so wrapped up in our own misery, that we often don't realize how many people are going through the same things. As the saying goes, "It always happens to the nice ones." Well that's not etched in stone, and it doesn't have to be that way.

I'm sure there have been many times when you feel everyone but you has a star shining over them. Problems of all kinds seem to surround you. Well, you're not alone. There are many of us who strive for higher ground, but find ourselves being challenged by those who wish us to remain stagnate.

The Grinch That Pinched

I distinctly remember as a young kid in grade school, first grade as a matter of fact, I was a quiet, shy, chubby little girl who always minded her own business. I basically kept to myself.

At that time, we had assigned seats. Every single day upon arriving to Ms. Fuller's class, I would have to face what I thought then was the brutality of a classmate who constantly pinched me. I never told the teacher, but in between crying sessions, I constantly asked Brenda Allen to stop pinching me. She knew that because I was a quiet person, who constantly put up with the anguish, she pretty much had me intimidated. She always managed to do this when Ms. Fuller wasn't in the room. At that time, I was afraid to let Ms. Fuller know what was happening. She may have separated us, but Brenda probably would have found another way to get me.

What she didn't know was that I had begun to build up anger and that one day I would release that anger. How I would release that anger, I wasn't sure. So one day after many weeks of pain, I finally decided I had had enough. That was the last time she was going to hurt me. One day as Brenda proceeded to perform her daily ritual, I stood up and said to her, "I asked you to stop pinching me," and as I was speaking, I got up and dumped her from her desk and dropped the desk on top of her. Of course, Ms. Fuller wasn't around at the time. However, from that day on, I never had any more problems with Brenda.

From that day on, I vowed that I would speak up when someone did something I didn't like. I decided that from then on, if the problem persisted without concern for my feelings, I would, whenever possible, distance myself from those who felt they could take advantage of me just because I had a nice demeanor. It seemed to me during that time that I was the only kid not having fun.

As the years passed, and I grew older and wiser, I began to realize other people like myself were being used and taken advantage of. It was difficult for me to understand how someone could possibly use another person to their advantage or for their personal gain.

Sometimes we allow the emotional and physical pain which people inflict upon us to linger too long. If there are no complicated ties that bind you, then there's no reason to allow yourself to be mentally, emotionally or physically impaired.

Even if there are more serious issues involved, there must be some way to break free. I'll be the first to admit, through previous experiences, that it is not always easy to immediately break away from a negative situation. But I always maintained a sense of decorum and constantly focused on things I would attempt to do to make my life better. We can react to a situation either negatively or positively. It is our choice.

Of course, the earlier school incident was certainly not the only occurrence of my being the recipient of another person's negative behavior. However, from that point on, I managed to take action in a positive way. I went through life treating each person as an individual, not judging them based on previous experiences.

On the Receiving End

From my point of view, it is always best to treat everyone with respect. When an individual repeatedly displays negative actions or attitudes toward you, then they no longer deserve that respect. Distance yourself from that person.

Chapter Two

The Excuse Abuse

I call it a lack of accepting responsibility. We tend to blame others or something else for our problems, our negative actions and who we are, due to lack of judgment, common sense or just plain respect. Some people constantly use the "I'm the victim" mentality to avoid taking responsibility for their own lives. They want someone else to take care of them, which is an indication of laziness. Life's not a bowl of cherries, and it can be the pits sometimes. All of us at one time or another have had bad experiences, but that doesn't give us the right to use those experiences as a justification to promote negativity. We promote it when we knowingly pass it on to others. People who are serious about what happens in their life try to turn their negative experiences into positive ones.

Many people want others to sympathize with them but in the interim they don't make an honest effort to improve their plight. Positive change will only come with a positive attitude and the determination to make things happen.

Some people are afraid or just plain refuse to admit when they're wrong. They will justify their actions with excuses or find fault with others.

Then there's the person who constantly brings up the fact that their childhood or their past wasn't all that great. Granted, there are cases where childhood experiences may have been detrimental. However, in order to move on to a better life, the past must remain in the past. Many people who have suffered great emotional and physical pain in the past have managed to find a way to turn their lives around and have helped others do the same. After all, it is your mental attitude that creates your life's destiny.

Anyone who continues to use those excuses to justify using and abusing others, and continues to get away with it, know they've got a "sucker." If they were truly interested in bringing something positive to the relationship, regardless of what it is, they would own up to the fact, then make an honest effort to correct the problem and not repeat it. Some people will use these excuses or sob stories to prey on the sympathy of others and at the same time attempt to obtain a sense of "quiet and subtle" control. What they're doing is drawing a strong hold on your sympathy. There is obviously no sense of guilt and no interest to improve.

It is so much easier to blame something or someone else rather than to say I'm wrong, or I need help. Some people probably believe that admitting they need help is equivalent to admitting they've been defeated. Being defeated doesn't mean you have to stay down.

There are some who will even admit they won't change. When you hear these words, or it simply becomes apparent that the person isn't improving, then you must make the change yourself. A relationship that is not based on communication and the sensitivity of the needs of the other person won't prosper.

Have you ever noticed that some people don't want to communicate because they're afraid of compromising or possibly losing something they're accustomed to having? To them, losing it means having less authority or control.

In many cases, when you confront them, they offer an apology, but sooner or later repeat the same action. Just because an apology has been offered, doesn't mean they are exempt from paying the price for their actions. Sometimes, I think paying the price is the only way some people will understand the importance of accepting responsibility for their actions.

Of course, we all make mistakes. But some of us immediately look for a scapegoat to cover up our mistakes. Be reminded, that there's a big difference between making an honest mistake and doing something you know that is outright wrong. Making mistakes sometimes may be the only way to improve. However, don't allow those mistakes to be repeated. When they're constantly repeated, then they're no longer mistakes.

The question is, when are people going to stop blaming someone else for the things they do which they already know are inappropriate? It has certainly become more apparent today that some people use their past experiences as a crutch in hopes of gaining sympathy and to avoid putting forth an effort to accept responsibility for the negative actions they bestow upon others.

I'm sure many of you have and do experience the "excuse abuse". Every time an issue needs to be discussed, the problem always leads back to something someone else has done or didn't do. When someone tells you, they're not going to change, no matter how wrong they are, and there is no apparent effort to improve relations, then you should do what's best for you. No one with self-esteem and confidence will allow themselves to continuously endure use and abuse from others. If you don't like what's happening, make a change as soon as the opportunity arises, because it's obvious the other person won't. Sometimes we have to create that opportunity. The first time someone does something, shame on them; the second time they do it, it's shame on you.

If distancing yourself from people who exude negative thoughts and actions means being by yourself for a while, then you're in much better company for doing so. We must distance ourselves from those who bring depression, and disrespect to us without just cause.

I believe that most of us would like to take control of our own lives, but some of us find it self-fulfilling to control others through deceit, and anger, instead.

Many of us become so comfortable and complacent with others or our surroundings, that we defend, justify, or settle for the negativity that surrounds us. People will only change when they're inspired to do so. If they're not inspired, they must be desperate enough to want change.

The process of change begins when we come to the realization that there is a need to change. To make an outright determination against positive change in your life leaves no room for help. After all, God helps those who help themselves. To admit there is a problem is one thing, but to strive to correct it, is even better.

Chapter Three

Friends?

Friendship can be like a well, if you keep withdrawing water from it and don't show concern for the source, there's a distinctive possibility the well will dry up.

You see, the difference between a real friend and one who claims to be a friend is that a real friend is there to help you when you need help; they share the good and bad times with you. The other is there to help themselves to what you have.

A friend should "be there" when possible. It has to be a two-way street, not a one-way street with a dead-end sign. Don't forget, there's the person who will do you a favor, but won't let you forget it. A true friend won't expect anything in return.

A Date or My Friend's Health

It never fails, you quickly know who your friends are when you're down. Take the young lady I used to work with years ago. I've always known her to be very nice, quiet and a person who's easy to approach. I'll never forget while talking with Amy Reed one day, she told me she had called Helen Harris, whom she thought was her friend. She had asked Helen to take her to the emergency room one evening. Helen told her she was waiting for one of her male friends to come over. In other words, Amy would have to find another way to get there. By the way, Helen lives only five minutes away from Amy.

After arriving at the hospital by cab, it turned out Amy had to remain in the hospital for a few days. There was never any inquiry from Helen regarding her health. Within one week of leaving the hospital, Helen asked her for a loan without even inquiring how Amy felt.

I noticed that Amy became even more perturbed as she continued to tell me how Helen wants her to listen and offer advice when she is having problems. Whenever Helen wanted to call, she would, regardless of the time of day or night. But the minute Amy came to her for support, Helen would tell her, "Well, I can't help you, that's your problem". The very next day, Helen would act as though nothing had occurred and many times, would ask Amy for a favor. People like this seem to find refuge and comfort in using others to cover up their own inadequacies. As long as they get what they want, they don't care how they treat anyone else.

Amy has allowed herself -- far too long -- to be treated this way by individuals whom she thought were her friends. As I have told her before, "People who do these things to you are not your friends". They don't even come close to the definition of a friend. People with this kind of attitude and behavior are self-centered and are not going to stop doing this. You have to cut them off.

You have got to stop feeling sorry for people who show little or no concern for your well being. People like that only seem to relate to you when its convenient for them -- when they want something.

Never feel guilty about telling someone "NO," especially if they constantly come to you and ask for things. One way to truly find out if they're your friend, is to ask them to do you a favor. If they constantly put you off, or come up with excuses, you don't have a friend, you have a user.

I can't begin to tell you how many people I've talked to who've loaned money to a friend, and then that same friend will treat them as if they're nobody. Many times, they will listen to what you have to say because they're in need of a favor. But the minute that favor is granted, they become estranged. The first time it occurs should be the last.

My suggestion to those who have experienced the intolerable from others, is to assess the situation. If it truly disturbs you, then determine the problem and its cause. Come up with possible solutions and utilize the best one that fits the situation. Don't allow something to fester so long in your mind, that you eventually become outraged.

Nothing will change unless you make it happen. The saying is, "Good things come to those who wait". But, don't just wait, attempt to make them happen. The negativity that surrounds you isn't just going to disappear by itself.

Many of us think that because we've been in a situation for so long, we might as well put up with it. It's never too late to make a change. If you don't like the way a person treats you, and there's a great possibility that something can be done about it, then you make the change. Don't wait for the other person to do it, because it's obvious they won't. As we all know, life's too short to be unhappy when it's absolutely not necessary.

Sometimes we tend to want things to happen too quickly. However, I don't find it necessary -- although it may seem comforting at the time -- to seek revenge. Just when I think things aren't going to get better, the angels seem to go to work and perform miracles.

As long as we maintain positive thoughts and our actions are in unison with those thoughts, the best is yet to come. God knows exactly when to deliver. And when he does deliver, no matter what the situation may be, it feels like a weight has been lifted from your shoulders. So, whatever higher authority you believe in, if you have faith and believe that a change will occur, then, it will.

There are several ways to determine who your friends aren't. Many times, they can't seem to hold a conversation unless they're the topic of that conversation. They won't spend the time to chat unless the attention is focused on themselves. You must pick your friends carefully because there are so many of them who want to see you fail.

Run For Office or Move on My Friend

Wo Chan and Carl Pearson had been friends for quite a while; they both lived in the same condominium community. Wo is an entrepreneur who knows how to get the job done. A few years ago, he decided to run for office on the Board of his condominium association. He was successful in reaching that goal and was elected Treasurer. Wo is well respected by the other Board members because he was, and still is, able to accomplish the tasks at hand. At the time of his running for office, Wo had known Carl for six years. Every year, he was successful in gaining a seat on the Board.

During the last election, Carl decided to run for office. Wo began to explain to me that prior to Carl's decision to run, he did not participate in any activities in the interest of the Board. Because Wo was in a position where Carl wanted to be, on the Board, Carl began to undermine Wo so he could obtain the position of President. By demeaning Wo's character, he attempted to convince other Board members he was the best choice for the position. Since Carl realized the position of President was out of reach, he began using other people to get Wo's position as Treasurer.

Within a short period, Wo noticed a drastic change in Carl. He notice how Carl began to dwell on "getting even". Carl stated that he would step on anybody to get what he wanted. After the election, Carl was elected Treasurer. Upon his election, he began to speak to Wo in a negative and derogatory manner. He often spoke to him as if to say, "here you are an accountant, and I've got your job as Treasurer." At this point, Carl was no longer worthy of Wo's friendship.

As the discussion continued, Wo admitted that early on, he was making excuses for Carl's attitude, but the light quickly flashed on. He was awakened to the fact that Carl had been using him. The two eventually had a disagreement. Wo finally realized since he was still a member, he could not completely dissociate himself from Carl, instead, he would distance himself from Carl.

A few months later, the Board decided to expand its membership. In his senior years, Brent Lucas was a condo owner like Carl. He had not been involved in board activities, however, he was elected Vice President. Wo noticed right away that Mr. Lucas would come to him for information. When board meetings were held, Mr. Lucas presented the information he obtained from Wo as his own material. He also attempted to convince the Board during meetings that Wo was not knowledgeable of the procedures. As time elapsed, Wo also noticed another side to Mr. Lucas. In order to compensate for his lack of intelligence, Mr. Lucas had a tendency to yell. This was his tool to intimidate the other members, because he could not effectively communicate. Yelling was his way of keeping others from challenging his comments. On one occasion, Wo stated that Mr. Lucas made a comment to him: "You seem to be a nice person, but when you disagree with me, I see another side of you". This was another tactic Mr. Lucas used to intimidate Wo to keep him from saying anything. Consequently, Mr. Lucas would have the upper hand.

Because he had been through a similar situation, Wo quickly realized what was taking place and made the decision to not only to distance himself, but also to speak to Mr. Lucas about the problem.

The bottom line is, Wo learned from past experience, and he made an attempt to correct the problem.

A Wolf Undercover

Sometime ago, Bernice Appleton was introduced to Dave Thomas by some of her associates. He seemed to be a very nice person, but as we all know, people are often not what they seem to be. You never know someone until you spend some time with them.

When Bernice first began to talk with him, he stated that he wanted to improve himself spiritually, mentally, physically, and financially. Within a short period of time, his actions proved otherwise.

As time passed, Bernice began to notice a pattern. Whenever there was an issue to be discussed, Dave constantly used the excuse that his childhood had not been the best it could have been, however, he never went into details.

There are thousands of people whose childhood may have been less than average. But they are making a diligent effort to put the past behind them to make a better life for themselves. They don't use their past to play on the sympathy of others and expect others to live their life for them by doing things they can and should be doing for themselves.

If this wasn't the excuse, there was always something else. Very seldom did he ever accept responsibility for his own actions. But because Bernice didn't strongly acknowledge that fact, he thought he had control and that nothing was going to change. On several occasions he never failed to say "not that I'm using this as an excuse, but..." The bottom line is, he was using it as an excuse.

Bernice noticed that he was the type of person who would spend as little of his money as possible. Yet, he readily accepted and even asked for things from Bernice. For Bernice, the light began to shine -- Dave had people believing he was a different kind of person than he actually was.

Dave often asked for things and promised to pay Bernice later, knowing that he really wouldn't. This proved to be correct on a couple of occasions.

Dave never inquired if Bernice had enough money at the time he asked for anything, which painted the picture that he was more interested in himself. Dave assumed and was self-assured that Bernice was going to constantly provide things and do for him upon his request. It was always, "Can you...?" Whenever Bernice asked him to help pay for the things he asked her for up front, he immediately acquired a negative attitude. When he came by late one evening to pick up a dish he had repeatedly asked her to prepare, he did not offer any to Bernice. He walked right out the door. Though Bernice did not fall into the trap of providing him with everything he asked for, whenever he thought he could get away with it, he would ask again.

This is the kind of selfishness, among other things, that continued through his actions and words. He would call her two to three times a day, practically every day. Many times she would be asleep. But instead of showing some consideration, he would continue to talk.

Because I have known Bernice for many years, I knew she was the type of person who, when she came to your home, and saw you doing something, would always ask if you needed help with it. Sometimes, she wouldn't ask; she would just jump in and begin to help out. Obviously, Dave also realized her good nature and began to use it to his advantage.

Dave did have some good points -- but it seemed as if they were being used in the wrong way. On occasion he would volunteer to do simple things for her, however, Bernice would always pitch in and help. She never asked him to do anything, he always volunteered. It almost seemed as if he was offering to do things in hopes of getting something of greater value in return. They'd go to the movies and dinner. On some occasions, Bernice paid, so everything was not at his expense. Bernice determined that, she would not allow herself to be used and taken for granted just because he offered to do things once in a while which she could do for herself. After all, these things were being taken care of before they met. Whether he was around or not, they were being done. It occurred to Bernice that Dave's attitude was, "I've done something for you, now what are you going to do for me?"

Bernice offered to help and work with him as a team. She over-extended herself to someone who claimed to want to make a better life for himself. In reality, he was looking for someone to do for him, while he did as little as possible.

Bernice mentioned to him that if his past was affecting him in such a negative manner, she would be there for him and provide moral support when he needed it. However, he must first determine that he needed and wanted help and would make an effort to improve. His response several times was that he was not going to change. It was almost as if getting help was not an option. That doubly confirmed, although his actions had already proven it, that he was expecting a free ride. It was obvious that he was going to continue to use excuses as a front, (as long as he thought he could get away with it), to do what he wanted, as long as he got what he wanted. As long as Dave could get material things from her everything was fine. When Bernice extended her hand to him to provide help, he rejected the idea, but when she extended her hand with something in it, he had no problem accepting it. Whenever the subject of resolving his problems surfaced, the response was always the same.

She believed Dave thought she had a little more than what he perceived a single female would normally have, and he saw this as the perfect opportunity to get whatever he could. She also believed that he felt threatened by her ability to work towards becoming successful on her own, however he wasn't so threatened that he couldn't negatively use her success to his advantage.

Needless to say, the friendship was short-lived. Through his actions and words he did not seem to be as interested, as he claimed, in improving himself. He thought he had someone who would cater to his needs regardless of his actions. Bernice had decided that she did not want to continue current relations, or attempt to take it any further, because he did not show the sincerity. It seemed most of the time to be a relationship of convenience for him. As long as she cooked whatever he wanted, helped him around his home, and bought things for him, everything was fine. But the reciprocity was far below minimum. She knew that to continue any kind of relationship with him would not have a positive effect on her life.

After quite a while had elapsed he called to offer an apology and admit that he knew the things he did were petty. To Bernice, they were not just petty, but rude, disrespectful, and without just cause. Though Bernice accepted his apology, five months later was five months too late. You see, we all make mistakes. Some of us make honest mistakes, but others do certain things knowingly, simply because they can get away with it. However, just because we offer an apology, doesn't mean we're exempt from paying the consequences. The objective is to learn from our mistakes.

A person who truly wants to improve their life spiritually, mentally, or in any other manner, will not tell you their not going to change, because improvement can only come through change.

We all -- well, the most of us -- work hard for what we get. Some of us put forth that extra effort, therefore, we are more successful than others. That doesn't give anyone the right to expect someone else to provide for their deficiencies, whether self-inflicted or not. It is up to each individual to assist whomever they wish, but when it has been determined that their kindness is being abused, then the assistance should cease.

There are many people who will gladly accept the opportunity to do whatever they can on their own to help themselves become productive members of society.

The way I see it, apologies and excuses come a dime dozen, but it's your attitude and actions that really do the talking.

The bottom line is, when you feel you're not being given the respect you deserve, then you must act appropriately. Don't allow something to continue if it does not have a positive affect on you.

On the Receiving End

Bernice didn't like what was happening. Therefore, after what she thought was a fair, though unsuccessful attempt to assist in a process of helping him correct what he claimed to be his problem, she succeeded in removing herself from the situation. It had quickly become a negative force in her life.

Chapter Four

In the Work Place

Jealousy Without Just Cause

I'll never forget, a few years ago Debra Taylor was a secretary who managed to succeed at her job and was rewarded accordingly. She was, and still is, the type of person who gets along with everyone. Debra also interacted very well with her coworkers. Several years ago, as an incoming secretary, Marsha Graves, began to notice that Debra had contacts and knew people in her department whom she believed were too important for someone of her caliber. In her mind, a pion like Debra had no right to associate or network out of her league. What really set Marsha off was the fact that Debra was asked by top officials to provide detailed support for top-leveled officials, while she was not. She didn't want to accept the fact Debra had the requisite experience they needed and she did not.

Also, because Debra knew and performed her duties exceedingly well, her immediate supervisor suggested that she support these officials whenever the opportunity arose. Since Marsha was not asked, and in addition, did not fit in as well with her co-workers, she constantly made an attempt to make Debra feel threatened. She became the time keeper and often challenged the overtime which Debra had rightly earned. On one occasion, Marsha actually visited the personnel office to learn of a policy which could somehow keep her from receiving her overtime pay. She constantly found petty ways to upset Debra so that she could have something to report which would cause her to lose the professional standing she had with the office and the department. There were times when co-workers had to come to Debra's defense. Then, and today, she still thanks them.

As soon as she noticed that Marsha was going to be a problem, Debra began to create a mental plan of action of how she was going to handle things. She had decided that since Marsha wasn't going to stop her jealous and petty behavior, that she would have to do it. It had become a daily ritual. She had made every attempt to get along with her. Debra also asked her supervisors to assist in correcting the problem, but was told that they had to make an effort to get along. As Debra stated, there was an effort on her part. That statement made her feel as if she helped create the problem. As time passed, Marsha's attempts to crush Debra's spirits and professionalism continued. Debra made it clear to Marsha that she could not intimidate her. Many times, however, it had gotten to the point where Debra didn't want to go through the hassle.

She had already determined that she was not going to quit just because Marsha made life on the job miserable, but after making several attempts to rectify the problems Marsha instigated, Debra knew she deserved better.

In the interim, when Marsha realized that she could no longer intimidate Debra, she began to try to intimidate another secretary who was quiet just like Debra.

Debra always believed that good things come not only to those who wait, but also to those who make an effort to improve their well being. Therefore, by being patient yet reacting positively to the problem, her time had come. And when it came, it felt like a weight had been lifted. She did not allow herself to become enraged to the point where she threatened Marsha.

After witnessing firsthand what was being done to her coworker, Debra's thinking was certainly confirmed. There are many of us who try to maintain our ability to be nice, but more often than not, end up on the wrong end of things.

Eventually, an offer was made to Debra to accept another position in the same bureau across the street. She took it because it was closer to her field of study, and she thought it would allow her to exit the secretarial field. Just when she thought she could start fresh, Debra found herself in a similar situation. Her opinions or comments on how to improve productivity were not accepted. She was considered a trouble-maker. Marsha managed to persuade her new supervisor, Jenny Campbell, that Debra was one of those persons who knew too much and shouldn't communicate with those above her level. So the two of them put their heads together and once again tried to intimidate Debra.

Since Debra had left an office where she associated with everyone, she stayed in contact with most of them. However, because of her jealousy, Marsha managed to persuade Jenny that Debra was causing problems by maintaining contact with persons from her previous office. After a couple of weeks, Debra was called into Jenny's office and she said to her "It has been brought to my attention that you are causing problems in your previous office". She would not tell Debra who told her this, but Debra already knew. Jenny further said that she should cease communicating with them or comments about the incident would be placed in her personnel record.

Debra was not going to endure this unnecessary pettiness any longer than she had to. She went straight to those with whom she communicated and asked if there was a problem, and proceeded to tell them what was taking place. Debra, as soon as she found an opening, took care of the problem. Needless to say, Jenny backed off. The bottom line was that Debra was not going to allow them to continuously abuse her character, intimidate her or cause her to lose her professionalism. Jenny, without really getting to know her as a person or an employee had immediately taken sides with someone else.

Food Threat

Ellen Green, a woman in her senior years, is one of the kindest people I know. Out of the goodness of her heart, she often brings snacks to the office for herself and others. Suddenly, things had gotten to the point where the staff was expecting her to always bring in food. If there was no food or snacks, they would even ask. One day she told me that when she arrived at work and proceeded to sit at her desk, she noticed a typewritten note taped to her typewriter. It read that she was not considered to be a member of the staff, but she was to continue to bring in food for them. It had the supervisor's initials typed on it. Though her supervisor had no part of this cowardly act, Ellen took the note seriously.

It had gotten to the point where they'd constantly search her desk for food, and would eat it if they found it. They would eat what Ellen brought in, but never offer to replenish it. She was never invited to any of the office parties nor offered to partake of anything others brought in, but she would be asked what she was going to bring.

It seems there are some people you can't treat with too much kindness, because they'll continue to take and never reciprocate. Even though you do things out of the goodness of your heart, some people expect you to continue. It's almost as if it becomes your duty to continue something that was once just a simple favor.

I told Ellen, "Just as they got use to you bringing in food, they'll get use to not getting any when you stop bringing it in." She has finally realized that they weren't giving her the respect she deserved and were trying to intimidate her through the note. Ellen decided that she would bring something in only if she felt like it.

A Devil in a Suit

As an employee who worked for the same company for many years, Maria Galvez told me she had never seen anyone like her supervisor. She's not the only person who shares this attitude in her office.

The supervisor, Melvin Dunne, had a strong dislike for Maria from the day he walked onto the project. In addition, he showed distinct favoritism towards one group of subordinates, while treating the others as if they were nobodies. They're not allowed to state their opinions, and their ideas are seldomly considered on how to accomplish tasks. In other words, whatever Melvin says goes.

As I spoke with Maria, she began to tell me that once Melvin dislikes a person, there's no hope. The office is divided into sections. For a long time, until recently, when complaints were made, one section was all male; the other all female. Melvin has made it known in several ways that he does not like women in certain positions. He treated them as though they were secretaries, and basically slaves, instead of the professionals that they were. He has often referred to female employees as "the girls".

Since Maria refused to back down from Melvin's attempts to dismiss her, she was known as a troublemaker. Whenever he was challenged by anyone who did not agree with his way of thinking, he constantly tried to make their life miserable.

Melvin constantly confronted Maria's immediate supervisor about her timecard. He would cover up the fact that practically all of the employees in the other section came in one to two hours late or left early but their timecards did not reflect those differences. Whenever someone else took leave in Maria's section, he always wanted Maria, or her supervisor to fill in. When they needed time off, it became a problem. It seemed that everything the male employees did, whether productive or not, was fine with Melvin. It appeared that most suggestions offered by male employees were productive, while the suggestions and comments offered by the female workers were constantly rejected. Male employees were rewarded for their efforts more than females employees.

Maria noted that Melvin refused to recognize females for their contributions. In his many attempts, Melvin constantly adjusted and readjusted her work schedule so that she would finally give up and quit.

There was one occasion when Maria requested time off for vacation several weeks in advance and got it approved. When it came time for her to go on vacation, Melvin, while shouting, angrily confronted her, and asked why she waited until one day prior to vacation to request leave. That situation led to a shouting match, which was what he wanted. He believed he had grounds to fire her. However, he was wrong. Melvin has tried to use his power and authority through his friends in the human resources office to back him up. He failed to realize that after working there for many years, Maria had a good rapport with many people within the organization. They knew that she was not the type of person he attempted to portray. Melvin thinks that if he continues to complain and attempt to make practically every day a living hell for Maria, she will eventually leave. He has tried on many occasions to upset her and make her lose her temper.

According to Maria, Melvin shows no compassion for anyone. It's his word, or no word at all. He is so blinded by the power he thinks he has, that he doesn't realize the majority of his people regret having to work for him. As Maria explained, they're all making a mad rush for the door. Melvin seems to thrive off of creating friction between his workers. He doesn't like the fact that Maria and her supervisor have become friends, so he has been attempting to divide and conquer their friendship. Melvin has shown outright hatred towards Maria and some of the other employees in her section; those whom he can't intimidate into being his puppets. Maria indicated she noticed that he attempted to "buy" some of his employees', including her immediate supervisor, by giving them gifts. They were then expected, and even asked, to go along with his schematic endeavors. It is very difficult to work in an environment where you don't know what your boss is going to do to you next, or you become very skeptical when he does offer to do something nice for a change.

He sometimes promised customers that his people would perform certain tasks without any prior discussion with them. In addition, he practically waits until a task is due before letting the employees know what needs to be done.

Maria proceeded to tell me that regardless of what it is, when she did something he didn't agree with -- which seemed to be most of the time -- he would take it out on her. If Maria's immediate supervisor, who is a female, did something he didn't agree with, he would still take it out on Maria.

Maria too, also noted that Melvin seems to thrive on the idea of certain people not getting along. He has tried everything in his power to ruin the great working relationship Maria has with her supervisor.

Though Maria realizes that people like Melvin will never change, she refuses to let him break her spirit. She along with many others in the office, have filed complaints against him.

Human resources has also realized that there is a major problem, which is affecting the overall productivity of the project. An attempt has been made to gradually remove him from the project, but it's almost as if he refuses to leave. Melvin knows he has control over the project and he has gotten away with many things that ordinarily would be questioned. However, he also knows that his days are numbered, therefore he's attempting to do as much damage as possible.

So far, Maria has been able to stand her ground. Though she realizes that the atmosphere she has to work in is not very constructive, she has always tried to maintain a professional attitude until the opportunity arises for her to move on.

Maria knows that in this situation, she just can't walk out and find another job that easily, especially during these times. Therefore, she continues to maintain some sense of decorum, while attempting to create other opportunities for herself. Whenever possible she avoids contact with Melvin. She knows that human resources is doing their part to move him to another project.

No One To Back Me Up

As a teenager, Melinda had two years of college behind her. Although her studies were not completed, she was blessed to have been offered a job through a college program.

At the end of the summer, Melinda looked forward to working full-time. As the weeks passed on the job, she began to feel as if she was in a medium security prison rather than at work. There were four employees in her office, three males, including her supervisor, and herself. Melinda had an immediate supervisor, Bill Crane, who was very fair and understanding. However, his supervisor, Mr. Tom Grant, was not as understanding. Mr. Grant acted more like a warden than a top-line supervisor towards Melinda. There wasn't a day that went by that Mr. Grant did not inquire about the whereabouts of Melinda.

Melinda's position required her to visit other offices within the building to acquire official signatures. Mr. Grant quickly acquired the attitude that she was the type of person who didn't want to work, constantly walked the halls, or visited with her coworkers. Her attitude and work ethics proved to be just the opposite, and her immediate supervisor praised her performance.

The situation became so bad that Melinda couldn't go to the bathroom without Mr. Grant wanting to know where she had gone. She remembers on many occasions when she would be sitting in another cubicle working on the computer, how Mr. Grant would search the entire office until he located her. Sometimes she would even hear him question others concerning her whereabouts. Because Melinda was not sitting in his office, where he would have direct eye contact, he felt the need to check on her sometimes two and three times a day.

What made it even worse was that he very seldom ever spoke or said anything to her when he came by. When he did speak, it was as if he was forced to do so. Melinda not only felt as though she was a prisoner, but also believed this treatment to be a form of discrimination. Bill, on many occasions when she returned from another office, would say to her, "Guess who was just here looking for you"?

Melinda managed to look beyond the discrimination and continued to perform her duties well. The quality of her performance increased as she continued to work there. She had been on the job for a few years. Each time her performance was reviewed, Bill recognized the fact that she exuded professionalism and performed her duties well.

During her employment, Melinda realized that though the situation had soon begun to deteriorate, she would not quit. This was her first job and she was determined not to leave so soon. Since Mr. Grant was the top boss, there was really no one else to complain to, except personnel. She realized that if she complained so soon after being hired, she would probably have been dismissed. Therefore, she weighed the situation and decided to stay. She could handle the fact that he didn't speak and even tracked her down every day. But she decided that if her record of professionalism would be tarnished by his obvious dislike for her, she would react accordingly. And she did.

Towards the end of what would be her career at the agency, when another performance rating was due, Melinda's supervisor gave her an outstanding rating in every area of her performance. When it was passed on to Mr. Grant, he immediately returned it and told Bill that an outstanding rating was too high and that he must down grade it to no more than satisfactory. Bill did just that. After being told by Bill what Mr. Grant had asked him to do, Melinda became furious.

It wasn't until she needed the support of Bill to help her ease the tension, that she realized she was up against the wall. Bill knew that Mr. Grant was wrong, but refused to help Melinda. Somehow, she realized he would not challenge the performance rating issue because he wanted to save his own skin. Though he ordinarily treated her well, she noticed Bill had no backbone when it came to supporting her when there was a personnel problem. She knew he would either deny the facts, or make excuses if she tried to complain to personnel.

It was then she noted that her time was limited. Melinda realized that if she couldn't get the performance rating which she deserved, it would later reflect on other positions for which she would possibly apply. She felt she already had enough experience from that office. She could take what she learned and apply it elsewhere and possibly be treated much better at the same time.

In the very beginning, she knew things weren't going to get better, so she at least had a mental plan of action which she would follow. She refused to leave until she had tried other options in solving the problem.

Subordinates - A Higher Priority

Howard Rodenski as a manager in an office of a military medical center had worked in the office for ten years. Within in the last three years of his employment there, his working relationship with his superior began to deteriorate. He always believed in being fair and affording all of his subordinates the same opportunities to succeed. Howard always ensured that his work, attitude, and performance was at the highest level. He was the type of manager who listened to his employees whenever they had something to say.

Howard did not show favoritism toward anyone. For that reason, he was very well accepted by his employees. However, his superior Jeff Plott could not accept the idea that he had an upper hand as he saw it in dealing with his subordinates. Jeff felt Howard had more control than he had. As a result, the working relationship Howard had with Jeff went downhill.

Howard's subordinates consisted of men and women. He had noticed that the women in the office had began to attempt to turn their relationship with him into more than just a working relationship. However, he had the same type of relationship with all his subordinates; a working relationship only.

Jeff had also noticed the attitude changes of the females in the office. He felt their attitudes should have been directed towards him instead of Howard. Therefore, he showed resentment towards Howard. Howard noted the situation created great animosity which made him uncomfortable. Because he realized there was a problem, Howard made an effort to solve it by confronting his superior. Jeff denied there ever was a problem.

When Jeff saw Howard in another light -- in other words he no longer wanted to deal with him -- his performance rating of Howard also took on the same light.

There was one female in particular, Joan Crenshaw, who showed visible signs that she was interested in Howard. She took an interest in Howard the way Jeff took an interest to her. Jeff hoped her emotions would be directed toward him. Joan always complimented Howard on the decisions he made that affected others. He was the type of person who would attempt to accomplish the mission regardless of what happened.

Since Jeff was not getting the attention he'd hoped, he began to retaliate by assigning Howard unrealistic tasks. Howard would be asked to do things that couldn't be done or things that could be done but was told they couldn't be. Jeff's attempt was to set him up to fail so that the light would no longer shine on Howard. To further his attempt, Jeff would no longer allow Howard to attend functions or meetings; instead, he would send one of Howard's subordinates.

Because he had tried to solve the problem directly with Jeff unsuccessfully, Howard had to file grievances. He realized he could no longer work under those conditions. While waiting to solve the problem through the system, he was presented with another opportunity -- retirement; he took it.

Even though Howard realized he was being backed into a corner, he continued to exert professionalism. But because he didn't like the relationship that had began to develop between his superior and him, he made an attempt to do something then.

Howard could have just quit, but did not run away from the problem. He chose to face it head on by confronting Jeff. When that didn't work, he executed another plan.

The bottom line is, Howard began to attack the problem by finding possible solutions. Sometimes when we make an honest effort to seek solutions to problems, other opportunities begin to present themselves, thereby opening new doors to peace of mind.

Chapter Five

On a More Personal Note

There are so many of us who are used, abused, and taken for granted, in one form or another, in personal relationships. There seems to be less equality and compromise and more one-sided control. Sometimes we find ourselves dealing with problems which shouldn't even be problems.

My Way or No Way

Ingrid Krumm and Henry Shertesky had been married for a while. As time passed, and as many married couples do, they decided to start a business venture. While Henry worked for another company, Ingrid ran the day-to-day operations of the business.

Henry notice that his wife was becoming extremely dominant. When business issues were discussed, his opinions did not count. Things were going to be done her way. He eventually ended up financing the business. Although he had no input in how the business would be run, he was expected to financially support it. Soon after, Henry learned that he was totally responsible for maintaining the home. Teamwork no longer played a role. He attempted to communicate with his wife concerning this matter, which led nowhere. He finally realized that she didn't give a damn. In order to release some of the pressure on himself, Henry began to complain to his friends. At this point, Ingrid knew she had total control over him. Henry had never noticed her controlling behavior prior to their marriage.

The bottom finally fell out when Henry learned that Ingrid was having an affair. Henry realized that since she had become so controlling, attempting to communicate with her would be futile. To compensate for his loss, Henry began a brief affair.

After several years of what he thought was hell, Henry finally met Peaches Mandlo. As he and Peaches communicated about life in general, they realized that they could possibly have a meaningful relationship. Since everything seemed to be going well, Peaches asked Henry to move in with her. By now, Henry was so relieved to find a way out, that he accepted.

To get away from the clutches of Ingrid, Henry went home from work one day, packed his clothes and left.

One option Henry did not consider at the time was seeking a divorce. Had he had the opportunity to get a divorce, Henry would have had a permanent closure on that relationship.

It is very difficult to maintain a reasonable level of positive energy when someone is constantly extracting it from you. If the other person doesn't do his or her share in bringing positive energy to the relationship, then the relationship becomes one-sided. If you've got to do everything yourself, what's the point of having a partner?

A New Addition

Robert Henderson, a young man now in his early twenties, received a scholarship to college prior to graduating from high school. He did well throughout his college years. During his senior year, Robert made a decision, which I'm sure he now realizes was not the best at that time. He met a young lady, Valerie Johnson, with whom he became involved. Valerie was a freshman at the same college which Robert attended. As the relationship progressed, she became pregnant. During that time, they both were working part-time.

After having the baby, Valerie decided not to continue with college even though her mother persisted. She stayed with her mother for a while. Because she didn't get along with her mother very well, Valerie also stayed with her grandmother at times. As time elapsed, Valerie began to show resentment toward Robert in many ways. However, the baby was on the receiving end more so than Robert. Since Robert continued with his education, he could not contribute as much during that time. Therefore, Valerie purchased the majority of the clothes and other necessary items for the baby. While Robert attended his last months in college, his parents provided help financially and bought clothes for the baby on several occasions.

Valerie believed that she didn't need help from any of them; she could handle things on her own. Some of the baby clothing sent to Valerie was discarded. In one instance, Robert's grandmother sent Valerie a check, which Valerie returned to her. Valerie requested that Robert's grandmother open a bank account instead. Six months later, when he graduated, Robert was able and had begun to contribute more to the child's care because he was able to work full-time. Since his full-time position would not allow him to pay his rent, bills and help him take care of Melaney too, Robert got a second job, a part-time position. While he was in school, he stayed with Valerie's mother. Valerie's mother was not supportive of Robert and sided with her daughter, even when she knew her daughter was wrong on many issues. Since that arrangement did not work, Robert was able to stay with her grandmother until he graduated.

On many occasions when Robert visited the baby after school and work at Valerie's mother's home, he noticed that Melaney's diapers weren't being changed often enough. The personnel at the day care center which Melaney attended had also noticed that Melaney was not dressed properly and she was not always bathed. However, Robert noted that when

Melaney stayed with Valerie's grandmother, she was given much better care.

Since Valerie and Robert were not able to work out their differences, she threatened to keep him from seeing Melaney, and many times she would not allow him to visit. Valerie did not want Robert to make decisions regarding any aspect of Melaney's life. The only thing she wanted from him was child support.

There were many times when Valerie attempted to create situations which would make Robert angry, and he reacted accordingly. She would then be able to say he would not be a good father for Melaney. On most occasions Robert was able to maintain his composure.

After realizing what was taking place, Robert finally realized that he would have to have the courts make a custody determination. Robert wanted to have visitation rights and partial custody. He did not get full custody. Valerie told the court that he was indecisive and could not make important decisions regarding Melaney's welfare. She wanted Robert to agree with all of her decisions without giving him the opportunity for discussion. To her, if he wanted to discuss an issue, that meant he was indecisive.

While continuing to work, Robert intends to pursue his Master's degree, so that he can provide a better life for Melaney and himself.

There are many young women who would be happy to have their child's father participate in the rearing of their children. There are many young men today who show no concern for the children they've fathered. On the other hand, Robert, who is making a diligent effort to make the best of the situation, has found himself being portrayed as the villain. Even though he realizes there will be tough times ahead, he will continue to do what's best for Melaney.

Hell at Home

In the Welch's home, there have been many days and nights of abuse and disrespect. Janet has been married for many years and has children.

Janet has frequently been abused by her husband Herbert who destroyed her self-esteem and confidence. However, Janet has to accept the blame for this. She has allowed herself to be brainwashed into thinking that she can't be self sufficient. And because she chooses to believe this, it has become a reality.

When their kids were very young, Herbert verbally and physically abused Janet. Now that the kids are grown, the physical abuse has diminished. Herbert still speaks to Janet in a demeaning manner. He talks loudly, so often neighbors and passersby overhear his conversations with Janet. What most people don't realize is that Herbert displays charming behavior when he's among friends and associates but when he interacts with his wife, he protrays an entirely different personality.

In recent years, Herbert has attempted to make Janet's life more miserable by having his female acquaintences call their home. Although Janet's job doesn't pay very well, Herbet demands that she contribute to the maintenance of the home and he insists that she pay for new items for the home, sometimes without offering to contribute himself.

Janet frequently talks about leaving her husband. She left for a brief period of time on one occasion. She has called the police on several occasions, but that hasn't deterred Herbert's abusive behavior. Janet should have packed her bags and left permanently.

There were times when Janet considered improving her life by going to college. She would then be able to seek new employment which, in turn, would help her build self esteem and confidence and become self supporting. Janet's friends have tried to convince her that she can do better on her own. Janet has to convince herself that she can survive independently. She has had several opportunities to improve her skills so that she can become independent.

No one can force Janet to seek help or force her to realize how much better she really can be, both mentally and physically. It's obviously not too late. If she has the notion to often think of making a change, she can actually do it. She hasn't come to the point of desperation or inspiration yet, therefore, she remains in a relationship that will never allow her to become independent, to build confidence and self-esteem within herself.

Which Man is Best For Me?

Dedra has known Stephan for six years and is now his fiancee. However, for about the past four years, Dedra has been seeing someone else, Tim Brown, in addition to Stephan. Stephan's career requires that he travel quite often. He also lives in a different state than Dedra. They normally try to see each other on the weekends and holidays and at family gatherings. Dedra told me she began to see Tim because she gets lonely and often has nothing to occupy her time while Stephan is away. She also said Tim seems to accept her for what she is -- overweight, while, Stephan tends to remind her that she has a weight problem. One of Stephan's family members was overweight and has medical problems. Dedra believes that Stephan is concerned about her weight because of his relative's problems, but it bothers her to listen to him constantly tell her what she should and should not eat. Overall, based on her description, Stephan is the type of person most women would love to have in their lives. He's career-oriented, responsible, mature and gives her the respect she deserves. He also on many occasions voluntarily assists her financially, and he doesn't expect anything in return.

It seems that she is in the process of destroying that relationship just because she sometimes becomes lonely. As I continued to speak with Dedra, she began to point out how she was being treated by Tim. During the first couple of years, she said things were going well. After that, Tim's attitude toward her began to change. He began to pressure her to become more than just a friend. I told her that regardless of how much he pressured her, she should have decided what took place. So, she decided to take the friendship further. As the conversation continued, Dedra told me how Tim would tell her that she wouldn't find anyone who would accept her for herself; he used her weight as a factor in determining her acceptance. Since her self-esteem was low, she accepted this. Eventually, he not only abused her physically but also mentally and emotionally. She would often do things for him -- buy him food, pay for gas, and loan him money, which he never repaid. He had a job, but lost it because of his attendance record, among other things. This was not the first time he had been fired. Dedra also mentioned that he could not keep a job very long without leaving or being fired.

Dedra allowed him to come and go from her home while she was at work. On one occasion, while she was working, she asked Tim to run an errand for her. When she arrived home, he was in bed asleep. She asked him why he had not done what she asked. He responded with an excuse that he could not get the appointment, which she knew was not true, because she had already made arrangements. Tim hadn't shown up or called the office. She told me that she began to tell him she couldn't depend on him to do anything. During this discussion, he got angry and struck her several times, inflicting physical damage upon her. Her neighbors were alerted to the disturbance. They saw the condition she was in and wanted to call the police. Dedra did not want them to contact the police, but, they did anyway. When the police arrived, they asked her if she wanted to press charges. She responded, "No". The police refused to accept her answer and pressed charges anyway. They saw the injury Tim had inflicted upon her. It was obvious she did not understand what had just happened to her. Just as in many other cases, time and time again, Dedra felt sorry for him; that he would have to spend time in jail. She not only posted bail, but also picked him up. Dedra has lied to her parents and fiancee in an attempt to cover up the relationship and what happened to her.

I explained to her that she is the only person who can control what happens in these situations and she deserves better. She also stated to me that he used the fact that he does things for her, such as washing dishes, as a guilt trip to keep her trapped. I told her, "People of this nature often do nice things for you just to keep you hanging on. Anyone who treats you nice sometimes, but disrespects and abuses you other times is not deserving of your kindness." She also told me he'll often say that he was abused as a child, and he uses that as an excuse for his actions. She said he admits what he does is wrong, however, but he has made no effort to change. Dedra realized he did not treat other females he had been involved with that way, including the mother of his child. I responded to Dedra by telling her there are thousands of people who were mistreated and abused as kids, who are working hard to create a better life for themselves. I also told her that she is in the process of ruining a great relationship with her fiancee for someone who could possibly make her another statistic. I specifically pointed out to her several times during the conversation that she holds the key to her happiness, and that sharing it with Tim has been and will continue to be detrimental to her health, and eventually, her life. I could not stress to her enough, that she needed to make a positive move now. She has put off setting a wedding date with Stephan several times due to this side relationship.

Dedra had to appear in court, and she told me she didn't want to go through the humiliation of having others know that someone of her statue could possibly be abused by someone smaller. Tim has said such things as he's not going to jail, or that he knows something she doesn't. He's also told her that if he goes to jail, he'll never speak to her or see her again. I told her that would be the best thing that could happen. Tim would say those things to intimidate her or make her feel as if she's really losing someone worthwhile. These comments have kept her in the relationship so far. "The best and only thing she should do is tell it just as it happened." Just before the hearing, Dedra also noticed that Tim was being very nice to her, which she believes was an act to keep her from telling the truth.

The day after the hearing, he visited her once more. She had suspicions early on in their relationship of possible drug possession, and they were proven correct. On one occasion she found a substance he had left behind. At that time she wasn't sure what it was. On this day, he was using drugs in her home. She asked him to cease that kind of activity in her home, or while around her. After confronting him about this, a couple of days later, Dedra told me he left a note on her door stating that they should go their separate ways; they both needed help and should seek it. In the letter he also said he was going to get help so that they could become a team. As usual, it was just talk. She said he reacted this way before when she asked him to stop doing something. Whenever she asked him to stop doing something that bothered her, he would use words to make her feel bad or make her think that he was truly sorry. There were times when his words or actions made her feel threatened, and as long as she stayed confused and depressed she would never leave the relationship. People with this problem -- because it is a problem, whether they believe it or not -- will make their victim feel stupid as if what that person is going through is actually not happening, that it's the victim's fault, or they'll act as if they have no idea what you mean. These are all forms of control. Those that are not strong enough to withstand and separate themselves from this behavior find themselves powerless.

I told Dedra that he is obviously a very intelligent person because he knows how to control her mind. He wrote the letter to make her feel that he was sincere about seeking help, but also to make her feel sorry for him, and to make her feel there was hope, when there really wasn't any. He knew her weaknesses and was using them against her. As soon as she would accept him back, he'd continue right where he left off. She also made the mistake of telling him she must have a man in her life.

As we continued speaking, she told me that she had been upset the entire evening after reading the note; she didn't want to lose him. Prior to receiving the note from Tim, Dedra got a call from her fiancee which ended on a bad note. At this time, he was no longer interested in their relationship. At least, to Dedra, that was the way it seemed. She also pointed out how Stephan had a habit of telling her what to do rather than suggesting or asking her opinion. Dedra said she tolerated it, which was wrong, if that wasn't what she wanted in a relationship.

Dedra has found herself in a constant state of confusion and stress, which is beginning to lead to depression. I told her, I certainly don't tolerate or condone the fact she has a relationship on the side, but if she feels she has to have one, the least she should do is find someone who will respect her, just as her fiancee does. Physical and emotional pain is not the formula for caring. Dedra has been through two similar relationships. It seems that because Tim says he accepts her the way she is, she feels wanted and accepted, regardless of how he treats her.

Tim also told her that what happened between the two of them was her fault. It is obvious that her self-esteem is very low, and she knows it, but she can't seem to get a grip at this time.

I told Dedra that she needed to do something for herself. She could begin by not returning his calls or letting him in her home and, in addition, by seeking counseling the very next morning. I've known Dedra for many years and I know she deserves better. Earlier during the conversation she attributed her lack of self-esteem to her being overweight. I explained to her, many people who are not overweight have low self-esteem. She shouldn't allow her weight or anything else to be used against her so that she feels compelled to stay in a relationship that is harmful.

Some men claim they can't find a woman who will stick by them; when they do, many of them treat women less than human, but yet expect them to stay in the relationship.

Mistreatment of any kind must be corrected as early as possible -- as soon as it happens, even the smallest things. Regardless of how small, if you feel you've been demeaned or disrespected, then act on it. If it means moving on, then so be it. That is why independence is such an important attribute to possess. It is those small things which add up. That is exactly what Dedra has allowed to happen. If you tolerate the smaller abuses, that gives the abuser reason to build on that. Most likely these occurrences are not going to stop, but will increase.

Dedra needs to associate with someone who not only says that they respect her for who she is but proves it by their actions, rather than make her feel no one else wants her, therefore, she has to accept whatever comes her way.

Her dependency on men has caused her to be in relationships that become absolutely detrimental to her. Again, as before, my advice to her as a friend was to seek professional assistance. She must learn not to be dependent on any man or anyone to feel whole as a person. She needs to clear her mind of these problems. I told her that she must act quickly, because she is heading towards a dead-end. Her dependency on having a man in her life, and the two that are in her life, combined with all of the problems she's having, is causing her mental, emotional, and physical health to deteriorate. Her job performance has also diminished. At this time, someone is working with her in seeking the appropriate help she needs. Although she didn't heed some of the advice I and others have given her, I hope she accepts professional assistance as soon as possible.

A Good Relationship Gone Bad

As a young man with only a few years subsequent to receiving his high school diploma, Jeffrey Taylor was well on his way to becoming an active member of the working society. During his early years, he met Pamela Crown. As their friendship blossomed, Jeffrey believed they were on the right path to a promising relationship. Early on, during the relationship, Pamela became pregnant, and shortly thereafter, they got married. While Pamela was a teenager, Jeffrey was three years older than she. Previous to the marriage, Jeffrey had noticed a change in Pamela. She became very manipulative, by using other men to make him jealous. After the marriage, the relationship started going down hill. Jeffrey believed that the pregnancy was an entrapment. Pamela was not happy with her family situation, and he believed she used the marriage as a way out.

Shortly after the marriage, Pamela's mother and her brothers moved in with them. Jeffrey was now helping to support a ready-made family in addition to his own child. As time passed, things didn't seem to get better. One day upon returning home from work, Jeffrey opened the door to an almost empty apartment. It seemed to him that without warning she had packed up and moved out. He tried to find out what would cause her to make such a move without telling him. He always believed her mother was the cause of the break up of what could have been a great relationship. After Pamela's mother moved in, Jeffrey was warned by others to ask her to leave. He had also taken note that as soon as he married Pamela, her father left her mother. Jeffrey had remained puzzled about what was going on behind the scenes of the marriage. He wasn't getting any answers from his wife, and certainly no response from her mother. Upon separating, Pamela took their son. She left no address and no contacts. Many times during the separation, Jeffrey attempted to locate her. He had hired a detective, to no avail. Several years after separation, Jeffrey was able to get a divorce from her.

When Jeffrey was finally able to locate his son, he was greatly saddened when he read about his son's death in the obituaries of the local newspaper. His son was in his twenties at the time of his death. Jeffrey was thankful that he had had an opportunity to attend the funeral. Of course, he saw Pamela at the funeral. She admitted that she had moved around quite often to keep from being found. She told Jeffrey that she believed they could have made the marriage work. To him, during the marriage, things were happening so fast, he never had an opportunity to pull Pamela aside, to find out what had gone wrong. Now, Jeffrey felt she wanted to restart the relationship from where it had so abruptly ended, however, since his son was deceased, he felt there was no need to sit down and talk. Overall, After thinking back, Jeffrey realized he didn't receive anything positive from that marriage.

As time passed, Jeffrey regained faith in himself. After a long while, he met Kristine Daley, whom he had known a few years prior to his first marriage. She already had a new-born daughter, and was raising her as a single parent. Jeffrey believed their friendship was built on a solid foundation. Before long, they got married, and he adopted her daughter. This time around, Jeffrey was reluctant about giving so much of himself and Kristine was not pleased. Jeffrey said he believed the second marriage was one of friendship, not one of love. The marriage lasted for over a decade. According to Jeffrey, Kristine wanted a change. They sat down and discussed their problems. Kristine told him she wanted more out of life than what they had together, but it was obvious to him, that she wanted to see other men.

The first time that occurred, they ended the marriage. Jeffrey learned through his previous experience not to let anyone come between him and his child. Regardless of the number of men she met, he did not allow that to ruin the relationship he had with his daughter. Although the marriage ended, he is still friends with his ex-wife and still has a good relationship with his daughter.

A Marriage of Extremes

At age eighteen, Todd Buck became friends with a young lady, Carolyn, with whom he worked. They knew many of the same people, went to the same parties and other functions together. The two of them even dated for a while. After he was transferred, they drifted apart. Upon his return to the home office, Todd inquired concerning Carolyn's whereabouts, but without success. To Todd's surprise, after many years, Carolyn called him. Since such a long time had elapsed, she re-introduced herself. They often talked and began dating. Carolyn had never married before, however she wanted to marry Todd. Todd thought the relationship was going well and decided to move in with her. Shortly, thereafter they married. He thought he had someone with whom he could spend the rest of his life. According to Todd, after they got married, he noticed a 360-degree change in Carolyn's demeanor.

Carolyn quickly began to accuse him of being with her friends and of taking food from their home to his girlfriends. Todd noticed that her friends often made passes at him when they visited her. She had a tendency to be nice one day, extremely angry and sometimes violent the next. The situation got worse as time passed. Carolyn would give him flowers and cards one day, and the very next day go practically crazy. They were married for several years, which Todd considered to be several years of hell. There were many occasions when Carolyn became physical, and he often had to defend himself. Twice she threatened him with a weapon.

Todd has had difficulty trying to understand her behavior towards him. In the back of his mind, he believes her friends were at the root of the problem. Her attitude always seemed to change when she returned home from work. Todd knew that several people in her office were jealous of their relationship and her professional progress. They attempted to ruin the relationship by feeding her false information. She allowed these problems to escalate, by choosing to believe her friends.

Todd realized that being in this type of situation can really change a person. He is presently in the process of getting a divorce. He has learned that when people can't sit down and discuss problems which exist and attempt to work them out, there is no way the relationship can grow. The only way Todd could resolve the problems he was having was to remove himself from them.

Chapter Six

The Family Circle

Let Him Live For Free or Put Him Out?

Martin Brown, who is in a relationship with Amy Reed has found himself between a rock and a hard place. Tony Covington is one of Martin's close cousins. Prior to being unemployed, Tony owned his own business. Martin has always been a person whose success has come from hard work and the determination to succeed. Martin has owned and run his own company for many years.

Due to unforeseen circumstances, Tony's company went under. Being the gracious one, Martin offered his cousin a place to stay for free while he got himself together. The agreement was that Tony diligently seek and find employment, take care of the house and pay rent. Martin even went so far as to offer Tony a well-paying position in his company. Not only did Tony turn down the position because he was not interested, but to date, he hasn't attempted to seek employment.

A few years have passed, and Tony is still living in Martin's home free and unemployed. It seems that he has decided his cousin Martin is successful and is financially stable, so why should he put forth the effort to find employment? He thinks he should stay for free as long as he wants, which could be indefinitely.

Family members sometimes think that because "it's family," they have the right to expect something for nothing. As we all know, no one lives for free, and that should include family, unless the situation warrants.

Through the years, I've noticed that many people seem to believe that because an acquaintance or family member "has made it" or is a little more successful than they are, they're automatically entitled to reap the benefits of other's efforts, without any consideration or thought to the hard work it took that person to get there. Is it not the decision of each individual to decide who shall reap the benefit of his or her success?

Martin now finds himself in a difficult situation. Although his family keeps telling him that it would be wrong to do so, Martin wants Tony to leave. The bottom line is, notwithstanding Martin's unselfish attempt to help Tony, he has every right in the world to put Tony out. After all, Martin earned his success, and no one has the right to expect something for free, not even his cousin.

This is my Grandma, Relax

Jackie Branado, to whom I give tons of credit and respect, insists upon coming to work every day. Several times a week we chat. She has been working for one agency for many years. One day I said to her, "Shouldn't you be home enjoying retirement?" She replied, "I can't afford to retire", and I asked her why. She answered, "I have a twenty-seven year old grandson at home."

Her grandson Michael, with her approval, had recently acquired a roommate, John Fisher. John had been a long-time friend of Michael's. According to Jackie, pity was the main reason why she and her grandson allowed him to stay there. John could not seem to get himself together; he practically stayed any place he could: with his sister and nephews, and in the back of his car, among other places. In other words, his life was not stable. Early on, he made it known to Jackie that he was on parole.

Jackie, who is partially disabled, began to tell me how she, most of the time, has to ask them to do things around the house, which seem to get done when they feel like doing them. Out of mere respect, they should be asking her what they can do for her. John, pays Jackie a weekly fee to help with the purchase of food or other items. Although her grandson helps her around the house sometimes, he does not give her anything towards food or the upkeep of the home. If they're not contributing as they should, what is the point of them, at least John anyway, being there?

Jackie especially depends on her grandson to carry things for her, since she is partially handicapped. Michael and his roommate sometimes takes advantage of her. After leaving work, usually after midnight, Jackie has to go home and fix their lunch and wash the dishes they used for dinner. Here are two grown men, who can't seem to find the time or the decency to wash the dishes after they eat.

When they go out to dinner, Michael and John, who both work, don't offer to pay for dinner, however, Michael will offer to pay the tip. Even when traveling, they don't pay for the hotel, buy their own lunch or dinner or even pay for gas. Who pays for it, Grandma. I could tell by her expression that she didn't appreciate that at all. Jackie hasn't required that they pay for these things. If they offered, however, it would be up to her to accept or not to accept the offer.

Jackie has already established a living trust for her grandson. He doesn't seem to have much money when it comes to paying for little things like dinner or gas, but he has no problem expressing his feelings through little gifts for his girlfriend.

Several years ago Michael's mother and great grandmother died within less than six months. Michael seemed to be extremely mentally disturbed by the loss, especially because his mother was constantly there for him and did everything for him. As Jackie said, she even did his homework. The county in which they resided considered

Michael retarded since grade school, however, he did well throughout his school years. He did not graduate because he was lacking one credit. Today, he does not have his GED.

Jackie told me Michael's psychiatrist has a totally different opinion. He believes Michael is not mentally challenged. He always seems to have the right answers. Although he visits the therapist, Jackie also believes in the back of her mind that he may not be mentally challenged. Michael has been visiting the therapist for several years. As I told Jackie, and she also agreed, Michael is most likely playing on her sympathy; at least some of the time.

Recently, Jackie made plans for a vacation up north. Thinking of the others as usual, she wanted to go someplace where Michael and John could find something interesting to do. She told them several weeks prior to start saving their money, and if they didn't have any by the time they were ready to go, the guys wouldn't be going. I said good for you.

If they're not going to help her financially, they should at least do more to help around the house. Michael, however, when it comes to helping his grandmother get around, and doing some things around the home, does his share. In many ways though, he does take advantage of her. She prepares food for him and cleans up after him. Jackie needs to be more firm in setting rules.

Upon returning from Pittsburgh, Jackie told me she, again, ended up paying for Michael's food and hotel. According to Jackie though, he really did earn it. He was a great help to her. Although he may have earned it, it wouldn't have hurt him to offer to pay for his and Jackie's dinner. After all, he works but does not financially contribute to the household expenses.

This time around, John did not go with them. Just before Jackie went on vacation, John began to disappear. He would fail to appear two or three days at a time. John had become involved with one of his friends with whom he previously attended drug rehabilitation. He managed to do very well while attending rehab.

John knew that Jackie realized something was wrong, so he decided to confess. John told her that he was using drugs again. He also informed her why he was on parole. He stated before his arrest, he was in need of money, so he decided to assault and rob a man in a wheel chair. A few days after their discussion, Jackie gave John his walking papers. She gave him a week to leave.

John later mentioned that his boss told him he was walking a fine line. Apparently he had not been going to work. The very next day, he told Jackie his boss gave him the day off, which to her seemed strange. She truly believes that he was fired. He was delinquent in contributing his share of funds for room and board.

Jackie also mentioned to me that she has had money stolen from her purse many times. On one occasion, she confronted her grandson, Michael, and John. They both denied stealing from her. However, when she called the police, they decided to leave the house for a while. After the policeman left, they returned.

After she returned from vacation, Jackie noticed, upon returning from grocery shopping, a large sum of money was missing. She questioned John about it, and again, he denied it. Jackie stated that John was the only one in the room at the time. She told me that within a few months she had several hundred dollars stolen from her, and her drawers had been searched. She noted throughout previous years that some of her grandson's friends didn't have steady jobs. His friends are usually there when she's at work. When it was just her and her grandson, however, there weren't any problems. She has spoken with the authorities on several occasions, only to be told that she has to prove that a specific person is taking the money. Jackie believes that John was not only taking money to support his habit but also using it to pay her.

A few days after Jackie asked John to leave, she caught him searching through her bedroom. When questioned, he stated he was looking for cigarettes. The cigarettes were within eye contact of entering the room. Jackie also mentioned that he had searched her closet. At the time this occurred, she was on her way to work. Before leaving, she told John to leave immediately before she left for work. As usual, he attempted to get Jackie's sympathy. He said he had no place to go. At that point, Jackie told him that was none of her concern, that she wanted him out. She was absolutely right. After all, she tried to help him in many ways. She said she was glad she was able to take a stand. I told her she was blessed that he had not become violent while residing with her. Shortly, after John left, Jackie noticed some of her jewelry was missing. One day, a friend of her grandson's and John's heard Jackie discussing the jewelry, and he said he had an idea where it might be. Sure enough, her jewelry was at a pawn shop. John had pawned it.

Since Jackie was able to take a stand with John, hopefully she will be able to do the same with her grandson, to get him to contribute financially, and do more around the house without being asked.

One mistake Jackie made was not asking John in the beginning why he was on parole. Had she known, as she agreed with me, she would not have let him move in. Jackie admits that she was feeling sorry for John, but she began to realize that while he was there, he lied so much he could no longer be trusted.

Since Michael knew money was being stolen from his grandmother, and he stated he was not taking it, the least he could have done was to ensure that when his friends visited, they stayed clear of his grandmother's room.

Jackie has learned a lot from this situation. I suggested that she should either cut down on the amount of cash she keeps in the house, get a safe, or put her money in the bank. Although she says it is easier for her to pay bills in cash rather than paying by check, she now realizes it has cost her greatly. Jackie also realized that by doing things for her grandson, he is not learning to be independent. He has become used to having others do so much for him. I told her, and she agreed, that when the time comes for him to stand on his own two feet, he will find it very difficult to do so.

Mom Will Always Be There

Mary Flann, a nice woman in her golden years, deserves a round of applause. Still a member of the working society, she manages to maintain an active lifestyle. Although she is not physically disabled like Jackie, she too deserves the right to enjoy the remainder of her life outside the office.

But Ms. Flann can't do that. Why? Partly because her grown children constantly borrow money from her. They never seem to be able to pay it back. In the meantime, they manage to go on vacations, and procure other expensive items.

Her daughter Terri constantly asks her for money to pay Terri's rent and buy food, among other things. When she doesn't get what she wants, Terri won't speak to her mother for a while. Terri has a husband who works, but she takes the position that her mother should help her. She becomes upset when her mother purchases things for others.

Brandon, a son, has a well-paying job. Until recently Brandon lived in an apartment, had no car, and bought few clothing. Even though he earned a substantial income, Brandon sometimes asked his mother for several hundred dollars at a time. Ms. Flann loaned the money to Brandon. He has not repaid his mother although he now lives prosperously.

It should be a crime for a mother of this age to be forced to work because her children won't assume responsibility for themselves. They constantly take advantage of their mother's kindness. It truly disturbs me to think that a daughter in the prime of her life, or at any age, for that matter, would selfishly increase her mother's credit card expenditures without concern for her mother's well being.

Mary is partly at fault here. If she had discouraged this behavior in its early stages, I don't think the problem would have become so bad.

But it's not too late. If Mary ever wants to enjoy life and have freedom from her children's financial demands, she has to realize that she is the cause of the problem. She must stop providing for children who can provide for themselves but would rather use her because she's available.

A Good Kid Gone Bad

As a young kid, Johnathan Kleever was a nice kid who struggled to maintain a "C" average in school. During his early years of school, he was prescribed a medicine to control his behavior and lack of attention. Once he began using the medicine as an excuse for his behavior, Katherine took him off of it because she didn't want him to learn that he should use drugs to modify his behavior.

His parents have joint custody of him. While in his mid-teens, Jonathan's father, Paul, began to show an interest in his son, something Jonathan always longed for. His mother suspected that Paul had ulterior motives other than what Jonathan told her. His father was going through a divorce and was facing another child support payment. He wanted his oldest son, Nicholas, to move in with him. Paul explained to

Jonathan that if Nicholas moved in with him and went to college, then his wife wouldn't be able to collect as much money. After Jonathan spent several weekends with his father, Jonathan started rebelling against his mother. Paul was empowering Jonathan on his road to destruction. Paul was encouraging Jonathan to meet him places and to conceal this from his mother. Within no time, Jonathan became more untruthful. His father was now blaming his mother, Katherine for their breakup ten years ago. He would tell Jonathan that they would all be a family if it weren't for Katherine leaving him. Paul stopped all child support payments. So, Katherine filed for back child support. When Paul was served with the child support papers, he requested joint custody. Within a year, she was now faced with numerous problems. Her son was changing before her eyes, her youngest sister died, her nephew whom she helped raise, was murdered, her mother was sick and her father and herself had to undergo major surgery. Katherine became extremely involved with the murder case and the other family problems and soon became depressed. This gave Paul and Jonathan the upperhand. Jonathan began to want to spend more time with his father, even though his father still did not show much interest in him.

As he grew older, Johnathan became involved with the wrong crowd in school, the crowd whom he thought was "cool". His attitude and demeanor began to quickly deteriorate. While moving up in his teen years, Johnathan had been suspended from school a few times for disruptive behavior. Shortly, he was heavily into drugs. His mother, Katherine, had her suspicions, but they definitely became apparent when she began to find traces of marijuana and other paraphernalia around the home. During this time, he was suspended twice. She constantly checked her own home to ensure there were no drugs. On many occasions, she found some.

While still in his teens, Johnathan was sent to counseling for his continuous disruptive behavior, including bringing a concealed weapon to school after a fight. He was not expelled because the Board of Education discovered teachers had searched his locker rather than a school administrator. However, at this point, counseling was not a strong enough deterrent. By constantly using drugs and associating with other kids with the same behavior and attitudes, Johnathan began to show disrespect towards his parents, particularly his mother, Katherine. He showed total disregard for home rules by coming and going as he pleased. Subsequently, he was charged with stealing a vehicle and damaging two others.

Katherine had many conversations with Paul and Jonathan to convince them that Jonathan should plead "involved". Finally, at the hearing, Jonathan pled "involved" upon the recommendation of his lawyer. Paul was upset. He again, wanted Jonanthan to stick to his original lies. The court ordered Jonanthan to the health department for a urinalysis and social investigation. A juvenile investigator was assigned the case and each parent was to complete paper work separately. A meeting was held with the three of them to discuss the problems at hand. Katherine began to speak about the problems in detail, while Jonanthan attempted to lie about several issues. Paul, as usual, began to lie about practically everything, including not knowing of the problems Jonanthan had. The investigator began to believe Paul, mostly due to the fact that he, being the father, even showed up at all. She had stated that most of the time the fathers don't show. She did, however, recommend, along with the health department, in-patient drug rehabilitation for Jonathan. After the meeting, Paul and Katherine each had the opportunity to speak to the investigator separately. Katherine took the opportunity and contacted her. She proceeded to tell her about the many lies Paul had told. The investigator admitted that she was impressed by Paul's presence at the first meeting, however, she planned to further investigate some of the claims he denied.

The arraignment for the car theft gave Katherine the opportunity to get the attention of the judge. Unfortunately, after she explained to the judge her son's uncontrollable behavior, Paul, right after, told the judge he could control him. The judge then released Jonathan to his father. Within 15 minutes, Jonanthan and his father were fighting outside the courthouse. Needless to say, Paul could not get Jonathan to go home with him. He remained with his mother a few more days.

Leaving his father's home after an argument, Jonathan decided to go to his mother's home. She wasn't home when he arrived, so he decided to kick the door in because he didn't have his keys. When his mother approached him regarding the incident, he began to shout that he lived there.

When he stays with his father, Paul shows little concern for Johnathan. He allows Johnathan to run the streets and is unaware of his whereabouts. Paul, on one occasion, knew he had custody of Johnathan. He went out of town without him, leaving Johnathan without a key to his home nor did he inform Katherine that Jonathan didn't return home from work after he quit his job. Of course, Jonathan wasn't going to remain there alone. Therefore, he spent the entire weekend in the streets until it was time to return home to his mother. Neither his father nor mother knew where he was during that time. Katherine confronted Paul and the only comment he had to offer was that he thought Jonathan was with her. Furiously, she reminded him that he was responsible for Jonathan. After all he had custody of him that entire week.

Katherine has found no relief through the judicial system. On two occasions when she received calls from the police, the officer told her that she had to retrieve her son.

She suggested they keep him overnight on the two occasions. He later advised her to lie and say she didn't have a car to pick him up. She also told me that the officer mentioned he had seen Johnathan many times on the streets late at night. It was obvious that he did not want to go through the appropriate procedures to detain her son. She has contacted many outside resources, only to be told she doesn't qualify for certain programs.

Katherine has made many attempts to turn Johnathan around. It becomes very difficult to do so, however, when his father, Paul works against her. At this point Jonathan sees his mother as the villain.

The only contributions his father seems to have made are mostly damaging ones. Instead of teaming with Katherine to find a solution to the increasing problems, he constantly justifies Johnathan's actions by telling him he doesn't have to be honest in court, or when speaking to any other authority figure. He helps his son avoid proper punishment by finding the easy way out. Therefore, Johnathan thinks he can do what he pleases and not suffer the consequences.

I told Katherine, "Johnathan at this point thinks he's invincible. He hasn't hit rock bottom, therefore, he thinks he can do what he wishes and not be appropriately punished." She agreed. She stated that she didn't want Johnathan to hit rock bottom because it may be too late to save him.

Katherine hopes that the in-patient program Jonathan plans to attend will become the turning point in his life. She is also going to recommend, that upon his completion of the program, he stays with her only.

Children quickly learn how far they can push their parents. While it is healthy to allow children some independence, parents need to recognize that boundaries must be set. However, what parents must realize is that talk is cheap. As soon as your children begin to show signs of disrespect for you, your rules, and create a negative atmosphere for others, immediate action is required. Parents should not only tell them that they're being disrespectful and disruptive, but teach them by letting them accept full responsibility for their actions when they get into trouble.

Parents shouldn't always try to fix the problem. If they do, children will think that if they do something else wrong, their parents will most likely bail them out and lessen the punishment for them.

Back and Forth They Go

Kelly Tukan, has lived in her home for several years. She and her husband Frederick had children, all of whom are now adults. While Frederick was alive, the family was like any other average family. After Frederick passed on, the children began to take advantage of Kelly. Kelly's daughter Lisa who does not live at home, also has kids of her own, but she fails to take full responsibility for them. Lisa has told her mother that she expects her to babysit. Lisa has a habit of leaving the children with her mother without permission.

Kelly's sons, Pat and Richard, still live at home even though they're old enough to be on their own. They don't offer to pay for food or expenses, and they certainly don't help maintain the home. Most of the time they show a lack of respect by speaking to their mother in a demeaning manner. Kelly has been trying, unsuccessfully, for a long while to get her sons to move out. There have been times when she's called the police to remove them from her home, especially when they became unruly. When she gets them to move out, within a short while, they reappear. Many times, Kelly doesn't even realize they're back to stay. Her home seems to be a revolving door, and she has never been able to get them to move out permanently. Because her sons have a tendency to associate with an undesirable crowd, Kelly sometimes finds trouble knocking at the door when she least expects it. On one occasion, the police came to her home to question her about her sons' activities.

Kelly finally decided she wanted to get on with her life. In an effort to do so, she decided to move. The sons feel that their mother has no right to sell the home. It's obvious that they won't be able to live free if they have to move. Therefore, they have attempted to create obstacles to prevent the sale of the home. For example, they refuse to keep the premises clean, and they constantly destroy the property.

Kelly has allowed her kids to mentally ruin her. She is being disrespected in her home. Her children never take her seriously. She lives in a constant state of confusion.

It is obvious that Kelly's words have no effect anymore. Had she been more forceful when the problems first began, not only would her kids respect her, but they probably wouldn't be living at home without contributing to the household expenses.

When Kelly contacted the police to have her children removed from the house, she should have repeated the process as soon as they returned, and possibly requested a restraining order. Although this may seem harsh, it was obvious that she wanted them out when she called the police.

Little Brother in Trouble

Before Randy was born, Frank and Lela Perry already had an older son a few years old. After Randy was about one and a half years old, his parents were separated. Upon their separation, Randy and his older brother remained with their mother. As Randy began to grow into his teenage years, his life began to take a turn for the worse.

Since the age of fifteen, Randy has been addicted to crack; he is now twenty-four. Since Frank was not there on a continuing basis to monitor Randy's behavior, he was not completely aware of what was going on in his life. His visits to see his son were infrequent. However, during the times he did visit his son, he would notice a drastic change. Randy as young kid was heavy. Frank began to see that little Randy was losing weight rapidly. But because he was not constantly informed by his then ex-wife, Frank thought that maybe it was part of his maturing stage. She did not want to acknowledge to Frank that there was an increasing problem and that she couldn't handle it alone. She claimed she knew how to raise them.

In addition to his weight loss though, his father had also noticed that his son just didn't seem healthy; his skin was very pale. His father had received a report that Randy was not attending school on a regular basis. He was receiving failing grades. But because all information was being sent to her, nothing was being translated or filtered to Frank. Whenever he'd call, Randy would be home. He managed to cover up his problems by saying he didn't feel well. His father then began to realize that something was wrong. Whenever Frank came by to pick up his son, Randy was very seldom there. Lela, though she had several opportunities, never mentioned to Frank that money was being stolen from the home, in addition to other problems. As time progressed, Randy became violent. He began to physically and more so verbally abused his mother; still Lela never said anything, which gave Frank the idea that everything was fine. Finally, the oldest son Ray spoke up and told his father there were problems that needed urgent attention. After Ray opened the door for discussion, Lela gradually began to talk about the problems she was having with Randy.

Frank had suggested that Randy stay with him, so that he could have some discipline in his life. However, not to his surprise, Frank knew he would have a fight on his hands. Randy did not like the idea because he knew he would not be able to lead the life he had been and he didn't want to follow his father's rules. His father refused to become a co-dependent to his son's lifestyle. Randy knew he could get away with anything while living with his mother. In addition, Lela didn't want her youngest son to leave home. On the contrary, Randy stayed with his father.

Since Randy by then had reached the age where he should have graduated, his father registered him for the GED. After completion, Frank enrolled his son in college and helped him find employment. Because Randy didn't like the idea of staying with his father anyway, he managed to find ways to elude him whenever possible. Randy had his pay checks mailed to his mother's address thereby giving him the opportunity to go back to his acquaintances and drug sources. He also claimed he wanted to spend the weekends at his mother's. But that was just another excuse to support his habit. His father had also noticed that when he went home to his mother, in less than two days Randy would be broke. Then, he knew how to call his father -- he needed money. Even at that time, Frank had no idea that his son was addicted to drugs, because everything was kept from him. He couldn't understand where his son's money was going. Randy would always have an alibi. So finally, Frank had requested that Randy's checks be mailed to his father's address.

His father requested that he relinquish some of his pay every payday, to instill in his son some sense of responsibility. Frank saved the money he received from his son for his education. However, Randy was determined to use the money for other purposes. On one occasion Randy's father had gone to a meeting, but left his briefcase at home with money in it including his son's. After returning, he had noticed that some of the money was missing; his son's portion. Randy was not there at the time. His father proceeded to search for him unsuccessfully. Randy did not return home that night. Frank learned through his ex-wife that Randy had telephoned her and told her he had taken the money; that he also had a drug problem and needed help.

This was the first time his son admitted he needed help. After inquiring at several rehabilitation centers, Frank finally located a center in Pennsylvania. When Frank finally had the opportunity one day to approach his son at home, he had noticed that Randy had been smoking all night. Two days later he arranged to have his son sent to Pennsylvania for 42 days so that he could cleanse his system and his mind. In addition to his drug problem, Randy was also addicted to alcohol. After being at the center for a few days, Frank finally realized his son had an addiction. While there, Frank had the opportunity to converse with other recipients who had the same and other kinds of addictions, but were very successful in turning themselves into productive citizens, both to benefit themselves and others. He also realized that there's a lot that needs to be done through education to help the weak at heart and mind stay strong.

It was obvious that Randy's cry for help was not sincere. The very same night of the day he completed the program, Frank went back on crack. Randy no longer wanted to stay with his father and went back to his mother. After leaving the rehabilitation center in Pennsylvania, Randy had also been incarcerated in Maryland. Frank's oldest son Ray offered to help his brother while he was in Pennsylvania, but instead of using Ray's assistance to help guide himself to a better life, Randy began taking money from Ray. He also stole his car, and threaten someone with a zip gun. After an honest effort, Ray finally realized that he couldn't handle him anymore. Ray was the just the opposite of his younger brother. He has pledged a fraternity, moved into a home and has made a successful life for himself.

At this point, his mother didn't want him back with her either. Therefore, again, as a father who was interested in the welfare and well-being of his son, Frank made another effort to help his son. He arranged for Randy to spend some time with his older brother Ted, who was a corrections officer in South Carolina. Frank again, hoped that maybe this would help his son clear his addiction.

Randy became so desperate to feed his habit, that once again he stole Ted's van which had little gas at the time and also took ten dollars to buy crack. Even though being addicted to drugs is dangerous, he made an even more dangerous attempt by attempting to deceive the sellers into thinking he paid them what they wanted, when it was actually much less. Before Randy bought the drugs, he folded the ten dollars so that it appeared to be more. While attempting to flea the scene, the van began to run out of gas. When the sellers caught on, they began shooting at the van. In the meantime, after fleeing, he manage to hold up a convenience store. Later, Ted was notified that his van was used in a robbery of a convenience store.

Whether Randy realized it or not, this was the beginning of the end of his destructive behavior to himself and others, at least for a long while. Before being sentenced,

Randy spent six months in jail. Upon arrival in court, Randy pleaded guilty and let the judge determine his sentence. His father and mother had asked the court to have him placed in a facility where he could get help. He was sentenced to reside in the federal corrections center in South Carolina. Randy was sentenced to ten years of which he must serve at least three years before being eligible for parole. Since he has been incarcerated, his mother has been reluctant to visit him because she doesn't want to see him in that type of surrounding. She has decided to visit him together with his father later this year. As the conversation began to end, Frank told me that he has seen a positive change in his son and believes that it's a change for the better. A while ago, Randy wrote his father. In his letter, he acknowledged the fact that what his father had been telling him all along was right. Randy has also decided to become a comedian and is presently writing material. His father wants him to further his education by attending courses at the University of South Carolina through the penal system.

It almost seemed that Randy wanted to live a life of crime. He was offered help both professionally and through his family. Somehow Randy failed to realize the opportunities he had been given.

Here, a father who was interested in the well-being of his children found himself being left out of the realm of communication. At the point when Randy had turned 18 or older, his father could have let him go without intervention. However, being the supportive father he was, when he became aware that there was a problem, Frank immediately began to seek solutions that would help Randy become the person he knew he could be. His father chose to stand by him.

However, Randy as an adult had to come to a realization within himself that he could turn his life around. Unfortunately, he had to learn the hard way. It took him longer than his parents had hoped. Hopefully, he will have benefited in a positive manner.

Chapter Seven

Relations of Reality

Teamwork, communication and respect for oneself and others is the key that will determine the success of any relationship, whether it be a business, friend, family, or a personal relationship.

If we continue to take and seldom reciprocate, there's going to be animosity and division. So many of us want something for nothing or as less as possible. Today there seems to be much less caring and more concentration on "ME" and what can YOU do for "ME". They want to get to you before you get to them. Many of us tend to judge others, to draw attention away from our own faults.

So many people are bent on taking back in their current relationship what they lost in a previous relationship. They don't feel redeemed unless they give someone else the same treatment. They feel that because they've been "done unto", they can't have closure unless they "do unto". This reaction leads to a vicious circle.

We should never go into a relationship of any kind directing our actions, thoughts, and words towards a person based on previous experiences, when they're are negative. We must learn to treat each person as a separate entity and as an individual, and not classify them as a specific element of a group. Then, based on previous experience, once you determine that the same type of pattern is beginning to occur, make an effort to correct it. If it persists, then you attempt to remove yourself from the problem. Just remember, you can't think and be positive when you make time for resentment or hatred. Each individual is different until otherwise realized. Every person deserves to be treated kindly, but when it becomes apparent they're no longer deserving of your kindness, then make it known to them that you don't like what's happening and, if necessary, find a way to correct the problem. If it means severing the relationship or removing yourself from the problem, then do so.

Some of us don't give much thought to what we say or do when we involve others, until its time to pay the consequences. Then we become apologetic. We don't stop to think how we would react if we were on the receiving end. You see, thinking requires a lot of work. When we think about something, we tend to weigh the pros and cons, and we eventually come to a conclusion on what is the right or the wrong way, or at least the appropriate way.

Then there are some who know what they do or say is absolutely irresponsible, but they proceed anyway, thinking and even sometimes knowing, they'll get away with it. But when they finally realize they can no longer do so, then they offer an apology. In many instances, irreparable damage may have already have been done.

Sometimes we don't want to think, because we already know the action to be implemented is improper. We'd prefer to take a certain course of action because it would give us a sense of relief or satisfaction at the moment.

Offering an apology for an action you know to be inappropriate, lacks sincerity. Is it because you're truly sorry, or it is because you realize you're no longer able to push around someone and control them anymore?

People also have a tendency to think they're owed something. Some think that because they haven't had the opportunities to succeed to live the lifestyle they wished, that other's owe them something. No one owes anybody anything. Opportunities are not going to walk up to you; you have to constantly work at creating them. We all have setbacks that we must overcome.

Sometimes we have to be wary of those individuals, especially when they hardly know us; who volunteer to do things for us. No matter how minuscule, they're often expecting something in return. And, women, you especially should know what I mean. This is also true when it becomes apparent you have a little more than they. My theory is, if you're going to do me a favor with the mindset of expecting something in return, then don't.

On the Receiving End

There are also people out there looking for a free ride; and if you let them, they'll ride you to hell and back. It sometimes seems that the kinder you are to them, the less respect you're given. Many of those who disrespect and use others, do so for personal gain, or simply because we let them. They expect others to do and tolerate things they would not and do not tolerate or do themselves. And that, is the best definition of hypocrisy.

There are so many women and men who will put up with the "unnecessary" just to have someone in their lives. Happiness and survival first comes from within. When you depend on others and material things to make you happy, your happiness won't last. When you find happiness from within, then the positive people with whom you surround yourself, will become a reinforcement of your happiness.

I'm strong believer in "what goes around, comes around". It may not come back in the same manner, but sooner or later something is bound happen. And when it hits, it going to hit hard. After all, we should do unto others as we would have them do unto us. In other words, treat others the way you want to be treated. And you certainly can't tell me everyone wants to be used, abused, or taken for granted.

Chapter Eight

Break the Barrier,
Speak Up, Act

To have someone as a friend or mate is a privilege. Therefore, when that privilege is constantly disrespected or taken for granted, then it is a privilege to be lost.

Don't allow people to take you for granted. If you feel you are being taken for granted, speak up. Sometimes others don't realize they are doing this, and if they become offended when you tell them, they're obviously, not a true friend. If you don't speak up, of course, they're going to believe that's its alright for them to treat you this way.

Don't allow what you feel to be abusive or demeaning behavior toward you to continue for so long that when you attempt to take action you find yourself not having the courage to speak up, or when you do, it's seems to have no effect.

We must learn to recognize forms of negativity, and not just recognize it, do something about it THEN. Just remember, you can only handle a problem in one of three ways: fix it, live with it, or remove yourself from it. Sometimes removing yourself from it, is fixing it. You determine what's best for you.

Sometimes I believe that people who take others for granted, and disrespect and abuse the good nature of other human beings, either have no meaningful life of their own, or they don't have a positive hold on life. They are lacking self-esteem and respect for themselves, and they find pleasure in mistreating others, or they just don't care.

Failure to quickly recognize and appropriately react to negative behavior can and will eventually have a negative impact on your emotions and life.

It is better to find a solution to a problem NOW, or to distance yourself as soon as possible. I also think it is better to be emotionally hurt temporarily, if necessary, rather than endure the selfishness of someone who constantly claims to care, but seems to find every possible way to minimize your right to happiness.

Some of us who are weak at heart tend to let the minuscule things people do for us justify the overall negative impact they have on our lives. They will do nice things for you to make you feel you need them. Well, plainly put, the things they do for you, you can do for yourself, and that certainly beats being unhappy. You deserve to be treated better. Go after it, don't wait for it to come to you.

The bottom line is, you must decide which is more important, your getting a little more happiness out of life, or constantly accepting negative behavior from someone most of the time just because they treat you nice sometimes.

Sometimes we tend to allow things to turn into a pattern, then we feel obligated to remain. We tend to keep our mouths shut and accept abusive behavior because we are afraid of hurting someone else's feelings, while our own emotions are being destroyed. We tend to make excuses for the negatives things people do to us. In the interim, we allow ourselves to be emotionally deprived of the happiness we deserve. Don't allow the abnormal to become a pattern. It doesn't make any difference how long the friendship or relationship has lasted, if anything abnormal or unusual begins to take place, and it's in the negative form, then you should begin a positive mental plan of action and follow through. You don't have to put up with it. When we continuously allow someone to take advantage of us and disrespect our existence, I believe we're giving the other person the right to do so. Each of us must set a limit. Why be unhappy, when it's not necessary?

We must stop allowing ourselves to be unhappy at our own expense. Set a limit, be firm and stick to it. You may be nice and forgiving, but you're not a doormat. It's alright to be nice, but it's not alright to be used. People who get away with it, know they can. Deep down inside they know they've got a 'sucker' who will do for them, no matter how they treat them. Don't allow anyone, whatever the relation may be, to disrespect or use you at your expense. By the way, a true friend wouldn't do that.

I made the decision long ago that if someone wants to be disrespectful and abusive -- mentally, emotionally or physically, they won't do it at my expense, or on my time. If we all adopted that attitude and acted on it, I believe there would a lot less emotional and physical abuse.

Don't become a victim of the 'revolving door' syndrome. If someone has had ample opportunity, after being told, to cease a specific activity that you feel is constantly draining your positive energy, once you decide to separate yourself from them, then don't allow them to return. If you have to constantly remind someone to stop doing the same things, then there isn't much concern, or respect for your feelings.

If you truly want people to stop treating you as if you're supposed to be at their disposal, then you've got to set rules and stick by them. If they don't like it, then they don't deserve you.

Parents must also break the barrier and not allow their children to run their lives. They've got to start when they're very young. Don't allow children, just because they are children, to get away with inappropriate behavior. Some parents allow their kids, even when they're very small, to do things that are inappropriate, but they will say "Oh, that's cute". The only thing they're doing is allowing their children to develop behavior which will become a tendency as they grow older.

Karin Phelps, who is helping to raise her grandson, will not appropriately punish him. At less than three years of age, he is out of control. When he's with her, he will kick, bite, hit and speak to adults in a manner in which no child should. The only thing she tells him to do is, "Stop". It goes in one ear and out the other. Many people don't want to be around her when she babysits him because they feel angered by the fact that he is so abusive, and she doesn't correct him. Of course, his father is not punishing him appropriately either.

Parents, especially when there are two in the family, or even when they're not together, must try to stand united in telling and showing their children right and wrong behavior. When parents become divided in raising their children, the children will quickly know where to go. They're going to associate more with the parent who allows them to get away with the most. The other parent will always be viewed as the "bad guy".

Sometimes, when parents see a substantial change in their children's behavior, they tend to believe that it's just a phase they're going through. Sometimes those changes can be a cry for help, and other times it could simply mean rebellion. The first and most important thing to do is to try to find out why they're going through it.

Probably the hardest part in raising children, especially teenagers, is doing it single-handedly and getting the parties to communicate, respect, and listen to each other.

Because they are flesh and blood, parents sometimes become sympathetic and tend to seek the easy way to deliver their children from the trouble they find themselves in. They will find ways to lessen the consequences, but this is the time to show children that they, as parents are responsible for them. There are rules they must adhere to, and unless they comply, specific action will be taken. Children will continue to do negative things as long as they know their parents are going to get them off the hook. When parents continue to bail their kids out, they become co-dependents of their behavior. As they get older, children must start accepting the consequences of their actions.

Sometimes, I believe parents need to apply what is known as "tough love" to make their children understand that the life they're leading will take them nowhere resourceful. The children may not agree with them, or may even display signs of hatred. But later in life is when they will realize the true benefits of the price they had to pay. They'll even begin to realize that what their parents tried to instill in them was for their benefit.

It is unfortunate though, how many young adults have to come to this realization after, or while they're paying a stiff price for their behavior. They learn that it would have been easier to listen, and follow their parents rules.

A lot of credit must be given to parents of young children today who strive diligently to bring them up on the "straight and narrow" path to longetivity. With the many pressures of society, it is extremely difficult to raise children when they want to experiment with many negative forces because they think it's "cool", or simply because their friends are "doing it".

Chapter Nine

A New Start

As the world continues to evolve, it is evident that members of the human race seems to have less respect for each other. Will things change for the better? Your guess is as good as mine. But there's one thing for sure, there's light at the end of the tunnel for those of us who maintain our self-respect and the respect we have for others.

I know many of you have experienced that weight being lifted from your shoulders when you finally free yourself from problems that seemed to have had a choke hold on you. If you surround yourself with people who strive for, and maintain positive attitudes, it will have a positive effect on all facets of your life.

There are still quite a few us left in the world who will always remain good at heart. I'm willing to bet there's twice as many though who are willing to treat others like doormats if allowed. So, don't let them. There's nothing better than having peace of mind every chance you get.

It is up to us to determine where the breaking point is. Some of us tolerate the intolerable longer than others. But I also think some of us accept intolerance to the point of no return. We should never allow ourselves to continuously be on the receiving end of negative behavior from anyone when they don't make a diligent effort to improve relations.

On the Receiving End

All of us as individuals must learn to communicate diplomatically, to our friends, significant others, or whomever, that when we feel we've been disrespected and put down, it is not appreciated. If there's any respect for you at all and for the relationship, regardless of what type it is, there will be a change for the better.

When communication between two or more people doesn't work, then it becomes more obvious that intervention is required if the problem at hand is to be solved and the relationship kept intact. The sooner professional advice is sought, the better the possibilities are of creating a peaceful atmosphere.

There are two basic ways to rectify problems involving relationships when the individuals involved can't solve them. The relationship can either be terminated, or it can possibly be saved by professional intervention. However, everyone involved must be willing to participate and accept advice. Then, and only then will there be a possible chance for reconciliation.

If a relationship of any kind is worth saving, it is worth some compromise from all involved. But, ALL must be willing to compromise.

Make a new start; don't be afraid to seek advice from someone who could possibly help you and those around you get the best out of life. Just remember, your happiness in the future depends on how you treat yourself and others today.

If you treat yourself and others with respect and maintain a positive frame of mind, then the light at the end of your tunnel may not be as dim or as far away as you think.

Many of the individuals you've just read about realized their life was not as full and happy as it could be. Therefore, they decided that change was necessary. They did not and will not give up on their fight to be independent, free and happy; neither should you. Results won't happen overnight, but they will come if you believe in yourself and your mission. Yes, in today's world, life can be challenging but you have the power to take charge of your life and to bring about positive changes.

A New Start

Patience is a virtue,
we all must learn to have it;
but let not our patience
become a magnet to negativity.

When you feel your patience running thin,
use your faith to find a way
to soothe your soul within.
And when you feel you've been struck down,
let go not yet of your faith,
and you will find a positive way
to turn yourself around.

Don't allow yourself to become a pillow
for the harsh blows they throw;
you too have a mind of your own,
move on, and allow it to grow.

When you finally break free
from the negative forces that bind you;
your mind will take on wings,
and you'll feel you have the strength
to accomplish anything.

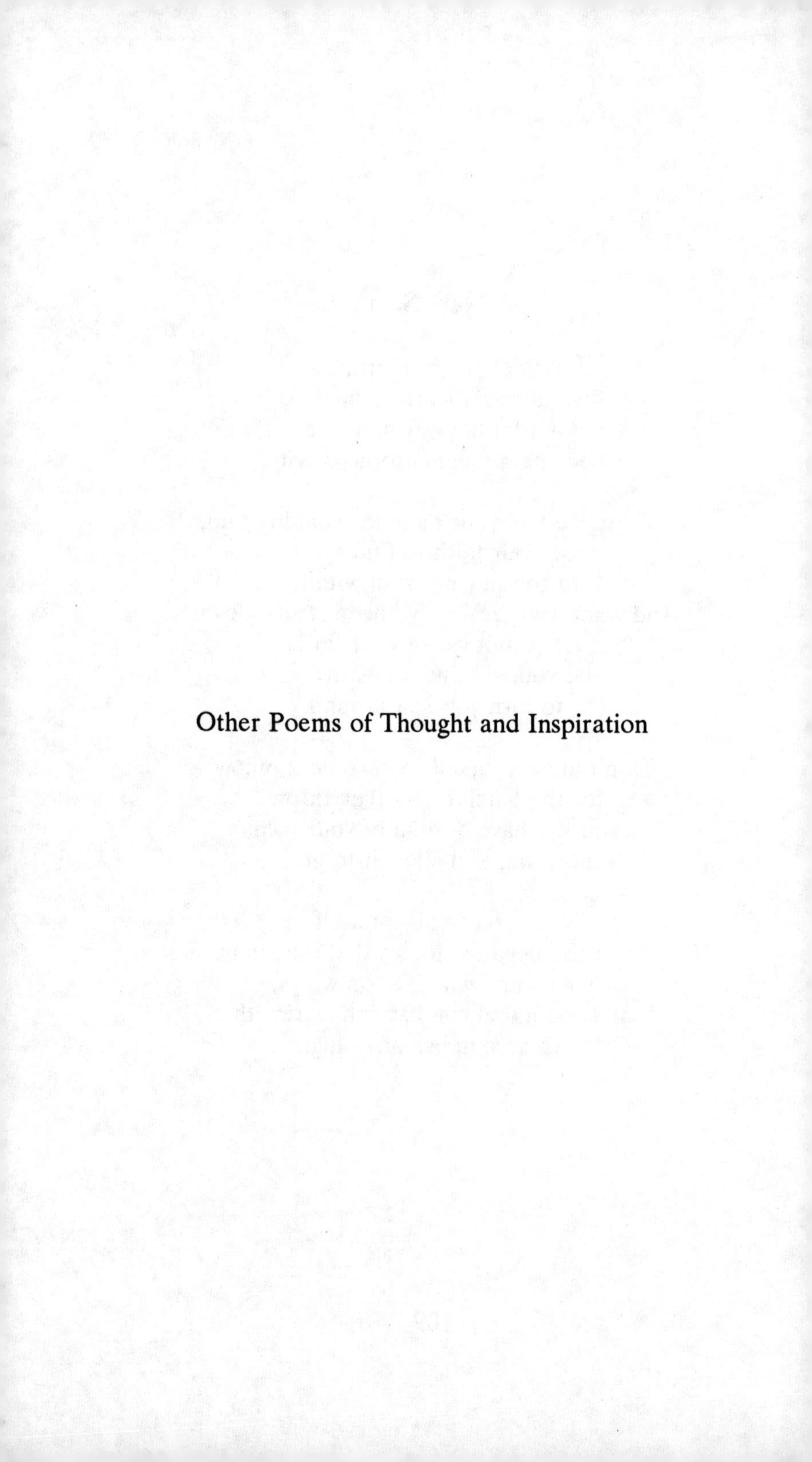

Other Poems of Thought and Inspiration

The Focus, the Plan, the Light

As we trudge along life's journey,
there seems to be a faint cloud
of uncertainty that surrounds us.
We see some fall to our right and to our left,
they've lost sight, they've lost faith;
they've given up on the Plan.

What is the Plan?
It is the pathway to our destiny.

Those of us who have the courage to remain upright;
sometimes, we too, begin to wonder what happened to the
Plan.

As we plot our destiny, we tend to leave out
life's trials and tribulations.

The further we go, the more we're pulled back;
as we move forward, we detect a strong current.
It feels like quick sand gradually pulling us away from
The Focus, the Plan; our Focus, our Plan.

The obstacles we face are like the ocean;
one wave can wipe us out.

But those of us who remain focused on the Plan
know one day that the waves will cease;
and we will see the Light.

What is the Light?
The Light is the final step of our plan.

And as we get closer, our journey to the Light
will be as smooth as a ship

that once sailed the same ocean which
made our journey seem endless.

As we begin to see and reach the Light,
let us not overrejoice so that we
forget to keep it lit.
For it is not eternal.
It must be maintained by our faith;
our faith the kept us focused on the Plan.

Endurance

Endurance. A test of faith, a test of strength.

As you travel through this journey called life,
your trials and tribulations will be many.
When the hills you climb get steeper,
just hold on to your faith, your strength;
and your passion to continue will get deeper.

Sometimes life is like a door;
as you begin to open it,
there are hidden obstacles on the other side
that keep you from your vision.

But endurance is what you must have.
The obstacles become a test of your strength.
Don't let the adversities of life keep you out.
Endure. For they're not everlasting.

Life sometimes is like a race.
Some will pass you by,
others will fall behind you.
But it is those who maintain a steady pace,
who will endure to the end.

Endurance is what you must have.
Those who sprint through the race of life,
may feel their faith and strength begin to weaken.
And those who fall behind,
may quickly lose sight of their vision to reach the end.
While those who maintain a steady pace,
are those who endure.

A Child is Like a Bud

To plant a Bud
and watch it grow
is like a miracle we know.

When we plant a bud,
we must nourish it daily.
When we do so, we reap the
benefits through its beauty.

Just like the bud,
a child needs to be nourished
and groomed for the future.
Your benefits will come through
love, respect and decisions
he makes for himself and others.

When we fail to nourish the bud,
it will loose its beauty;
it becomes an eyesore among the others.

Just like the bud,
when the child becomes
spiritually and mentally malnourished,
he begins to show signs of disobedience and aggression.

Though we may nourish the bud daily,
sometimes we are disappointed
when the bud doesn't give us its true potential.
We ask ourselves, where did we go wrong?

Just like the bud,
a child will disappoint us
when he strays from the daily
teachings of those who care.

When fall arrives and the bud
has given us its beauty;
it is time for it to fade into
a season of frost and chills.

Just like the bud,
when the child becomes of age
and he has shown he can stand on his own,
the time has come for him to walk
into a season of adulthood.

The Protector, the Preserver, the Creator

The Protector, the Preserver, the Creator. A Mighty Source.
The source of all beings,
to believe in Him is to have faith,
to have Faith in Him, is to receive his blessings.

He's many things to many people.
He protects us when its unexpected.
He even deliver those who sometimes
know they may not deserve it.

He gives vision to those who are blinded by darkness;
He gives strength to those who have succumb to weakness;
He'll straighten the path for those who walk crooked;
He'll pick up those who have fallen;
He'll give a soft tongue to those who speak harshly;
He'll provide for those who have not;
He'll give positive thoughts to those who think otherwise,
He'll shield you from those who seek to harm you.

To receive these glories is to praise Him.
To receive these glories it to have Faith.

Your Faith in Him will be the test of his glories.

The Mind

The Mind. A masterpiece;
when molded and sculptured
to focus on success.

The Mind. An ingenious tool;
that if used constructively,
can let you build ideas of gold,
and lead you to endless possibilities.

The Mind. A state;
that brings one to his knees in depression;
but allows the same one to be
elated with happiness.

The Mind, when refreshed,
can absorb enormous amounts of information,
but when fatigue sets in,
it reacts to words like water to grease.

The Mind. A time bomb;
that when triggered by the evils of society,
can lead your body and soul to total destruction.

The Mind. An intangible source
that lets you choose your destiny.

The Hand

Mothers

They know when you're happy,
they know when you are sad,
they know when you're in need of caring,
because, they too, often have been there.

They bring you love and understanding
when your heart is filled with pain.
When they find you're not in the best of moods,
they're there for you again, again.

Mothers have a special sense,
they know when trouble's near;
they offer us the best advice,
though sometimes we fail to adhere.

Mothers don't want to live our lives
they only want us to be independent.
If we often took the time to think,
we'd know it from the time and effort they spend.

Sometimes we wish our mothers wouldn't interfere,
but when no one's there, and troubles near,
how many times have we said,
oh mom, I glad you're here?

Let us not take our mothers for granted,
they too are people just like us;
for without them, imagine where we'd be,
nowhere, non-existent.

Praise

When someone has done well,
give them the praise for
the position they've upheld.

For when we praise one
who has done well,
we give them inspiration
to continue as they should.

Let us not find jealousy in what
others have turned into success;
but use their diligence and patience
as a format to do our best.

Let us take note,
we all don't achieve success in the same way;
so when you feel you've been passed by,
just remember perseverance is the key;
don't dismay, success someday too will come your way.

Life's Majestic Mountain

Snowy white, grey, black, colorful, peaceful, bold.
Solid rock, it's peak high in the clouds.
Deeply rooted, unmovable, treacherous when wet.
A challenge to climb, breathtaking.

As we attempt to reach the pinnacle
of our journey to the top,
we are amazed at the different
angles life has to offer.
Jagged edges sometimes deter us.
We must then find a new path to longevity.
As the rains of negativity challenge us
we tend to slip and fall on its sharpest points,
so we must become deeply rooted
in our desire to continue.
And because we've planted our feet on a solid foundation;
time is on our side.
When we finally reach the top,
the view from below will take us by surprise;
for below, the bottom, is where we began.

Now that we've reached the top,
let us not be become over-confident.
Our time there is limited, it is not forever.
We must prepare ourselves for descent;
for it is someone else's turn.
The way in which we descend however,
is in the hands of our imagination;
will we plummet to the bottom,
or will we descend slowly to a comfortable resting place.

Order a Book for a Friend

Please include payment with order.

Mail order to:

Especially For You
On the Receiving End
12471 Dillingham Sq., Box 201
Woodbridge, VA 22192

Please send me ( ) copies of "On the Receiving End" at the following address:

Name:____

Address:____

City:______________________ State:______ Zip:______________

Price: $11.95 ______________

Sales tax: ______________
Please add 4.5% for books shipped to Virginia addresses.

Shipping and handling: $3.00. ______________
$.75 each additional book.

Total: ______________

Payment enclosed:
( ) Check
( ) Money order
( ) Credit card (Visa/Mastercard)
Card type____

Name on card______________________________________

Expiration date________/_________

Telephone(______)______________